NIGHTMARES TO MIRACLES

Miracle Mindsets For CEOs,
Executives, and Entrepreneurs to
Transform Adversity into Success
In Health, Wealth, Love, and
Enlightenment

David C. Asomaning, Ph.D.

ISBN print: 978-1-7335213-3-8
ISBN ebook: 978-1-7335213-2-4

CONTENTS

ACKNOWLEDGMENTS

My deep thanks to all my teachers, students, clients, family, and friends who have encouraged and supported me over these many years, on the journey of creating this book and the leadership development program it is based on.

In particular, my eternal gratitude goes to my father, Dr. E.J.A. Asomaning, for the many lessons he taught me about leadership. My gratitude also extends to my mother, Sandra Cohen, for sharing with me her love of history and the power of American democracy, and for her very close reading of the manuscript in order to correct the many typos it contained.

My sincere and deep thanks to the Miracle Life (ACIM) study group: you know who you are; to my first editor, Gail Seymour, who worked wonders with very rough materials in a very short time; to my designer, Emily Armstrong of Starling Memory Creative, for the amazing high-resolution images in the book; and to Martina Tannery of MartinasPhotography.com for the amazing pictures from an amazing photoshoot.

I am also grateful to Brittany New of TheECourseGuru.com for helping me translate the ideas in this book into the online course, and for numerous other forms of assistance including with my podcast.

Many thanks to GermanCreative for a beautiful and intriguing cover for the book, and to Karolin Frimodig of SoPixels.com for beautiful social media graphics.

My deep thanks to Dave Pasquantonio of DavePasquantonio.com for powerful editing and formatting of the manuscript, and to Alix Sloan of AlixSloan.com for her expert marketing know-how to launch the book.

Also many thanks to Aleksandra Llalla of Temblor Consulting LLC for her fabulous social media management on many different levels.

The saying "It takes a village" comes to mind when I think of all these talented professionals who have helped this book come into existence and move out into the world.

Also, I am deeply grateful to all my reviewers. Your generosity, commitment, and dedication to the project have inspired and moved me deeply.

Finally, my deepest gratitude to You, The Inner Voice, for your constant LOVE and HELP in solving all problems that seem impossible to solve.

1 Thus will each gift to God be multiplied a thousandfold and tens of thousands more. 2 And when it is returned to you, it will surpass in might the little gift you gave as much as does the radiance of the sun outshine the tiny gleam a firefly makes an uncertain moment and goes out. 3 The steady brilliance of this light remains and leads you out of darkness, nor will you be able to forget the way again.
----**A Course in Miracles, W.97.6.1-3**

WHAT'S IN THIS FOR YOU?

5 Through the Love of God within you, you can resolve all seeming difficulties without effort and in sure confidence.
—A Course in Miracles, W-50.4.5

I think of miracles as solutions to problems that seem impossible to solve. They are solutions that originate from the Divine source within us. This is my working definition of miracles, and it is what I mean by the term throughout this book. This approach to the term distinguishes it from other understandings which include technological miracles from the wheel on forward. As we proceed through the book, I hope you come to find miracles as attractive and useful as I do.

This book is an attempt to put the essence of my executive coaching method into a cohesive, straightforward, and easily accessible format. While a book cannot replace the many nuances and dynamics of a person-to-person coaching process, I hope that this book does provide a clear road map for those interested in my method.

This book also provides an overview of what my online course of the same name covers. So while the benefits of this book are that one receives an organized overview of my method, one of the main drawbacks of putting my method into a book is that the things that I repeat and support clients to rehearse and practice over and over again, which can be exciting, inspiring, and accretive in the context of person-to-person coaching, can come across as a bit flat on paper. Nonetheless, I think the benefits of having my method in book form outweigh the limitations.

As we move forward with this material, which includes suggested inventories and exercises, please make sure you have a dedicated "Nightmares to Miracles" success journal (electronic or otherwise) where you can keep track of your thoughts, feelings, and insights along the way.

In the spirit of trying to be as useful to you as possible, I will now jump right into some initial questions for you.

Four Sets of Questions

As part of any new client's initial strategy session, I always ask the same questions to identify the client's needs and set expectations for the work we will do together. Before we dive into The Nightmares to Miracles Program, I want you to ask yourself those same questions.

Set 1:

- What are your top three personal and/or professional goals that you want to work towards?

Set 2:

- What are your biggest challenges in achieving these goals?
- What personal attitudes, mindsets, habits, and behaviors of yours get in the way of your accomplishing your goals?

Set 3:

- What have you already tried that hasn't worked when seeking help to overcome your blocks and challenges?
- Have you tried coaching, therapy, or other self-help systems?
- What did you get out of them, and what didn't you get out of them?

Set 4:

- What will your life look like in six months as a result of making progress on these goals?
- What will your life look like in 12 months after you've made progress on these goals?

Is Nightmares to Miracles for You?

I have a 16-point checklist I use to help potential clients identify whether they are a good fit for The Nightmares to Miracles Program. You don't have to agree with all sixteen points to get some benefit out of this, but I think it's fair to say that the more of these points you identify with, the more profoundly you are likely to experience the benefits of this program.

To make sure you are in the right place, go through this checklist with me and see if you can recognize yourself in any of these:

1. You are an ambitious and successful CEO, entrepreneur, attorney, doctor, financier, or other professional.
2. Despite your many amazing successes, you are still often stressed out and out of balance about your health or other aspects of your life.
3. You often feel disorganized.
4. You feel your schedule and responsibilities are often unmanageable or out of control.
5. You are often deeply worried about money.
6. You don't know who to trust.

7. You lack true inner peace and security.

8. You desire to make a much greater positive impact on the world.

9. Your legacy concerns you. This may be your financial or spiritual legacy or your business or personal affairs.

10. Your personal or professional relationships are often in conflict.

11. Your overall purpose in life is unclear to you. Despite your accomplishments, you feel adrift or directionless.

12. You want to do less and achieve more by leveraging your time and energy efficiently and effectively.

13. You want the teams you lead to be more cohesive, effective, and harmonious.

14. You feel constricted or trapped by the roles you play in life and others' expectations of you. The roles you have adopted may no longer fit, and you are ready to evolve.

15. You want to pursue new directions and interests, but you are feeling blocked and stuck. You may be afraid of the consequences of change or feel unable to initiate meaningful change for yourself.

16. Aspects of your life feel like a terrible, ongoing nightmare. You may feel insecure or powerless to move forward with your business or personal life, or you may be afraid of being found out, exposed, or attacked for something you have done or failed to do.

The last item on the list especially summarizes the feeling of nightmare that The Nightmares to Miracles Program addresses. The overall purpose of the program is to establish foundations in our minds that will help us wake up from the nightmares that we're experiencing in the various areas of our lives.

How Will You Improve?

If you complete The Nightmare to Miracles Program and implement it in your daily life, you will have more time freedom, work freedom, location freedom, and money freedom.

Time freedom means you will be able to use more of your time the way you want to. You will not be under strict compulsion from others to do things at specific times. You will have more free time to use the way you want to.

You will also have work freedom. In other words, you will be doing the kind of work that is fulfilling to you. It will not just be busy work—going through the motions and doing things you think you have to do, but don't really want to.

Location freedom means you will be able to work from where you want to work. You can use technology—your phone and your laptop, for example. You can stay in touch with people you need to stay in touch with and get things done. As a leader, you can lead from almost anywhere.

Then, of course, you will have money freedom. You will continue to set and achieve the financial targets that are important to you.

You will also reduce your stress levels significantly. The Nightmares to Miracles Program will become part of your daily regime to prepare for and start your day so that you are reducing stress right from the beginning.

As stress rises, you will have ways of reducing its impact. At the end of the day, you will have a way of preparing for sleep that helps you to reduce stress as well.

You will enjoy greater peace, able to reset in a peaceful mode after disturbing or conflicted experiences. You will also be better organized by working from a master plan that is constantly improving and therefore, that is leading you to be more thoughtful and strategic about everything you do on a daily, weekly, monthly, and yearly basis.

You will also live in greater balance. A big part of The Nightmares to Miracles Program is about keeping your eye on health, wealth, love, and enlightenment on an ongoing basis. By keeping your eye on these four "Doors to Miracle Success" in a synergistic way, you will find yourself in greater balance more consistently.

You will also learn how to do less and accomplish more. This is a key element of miracle-minded approaches to living. As you spend more time refining your mental state, you learn how to do less and get more done.

You will resolve relationship conflicts in so many ways, inter-generationally and multi-dimensionally, as well as in your present circumstances. As a result, you will be able to build stronger teams. A large part of this results from instilling greater alignment between members, so that everybody is coordinated in executing towards the same ends.

You will be able to reach and influence more people, and for the better. There are all kinds of ways one can begin to practice this without undue or unnecessary heavy lifting.

Your bottom line can improve significantly too, and it's exciting to explore what this could mean if we consider aiming for 10x increases. Just to be clear, 10x is not 10 times your current revenue. It is doubling your revenue 10 times. So, if you are creating $50,000 in revenue, 10x does not result in $500,000 revenue.

In fact if you double $50,000 ten times, you get the following:

1. $50,000 x 2 = $100,000
2. $100,000 x 2 = $200,000
3. $200,000 x 2 = $400,000
4. $400,000 x 2 = $800,000
5. $800,000 x 2 = $1.6m
6. $1.6m x 2 = $3.2m
7. $3.2m x 2 = $6.4m
8. $6.4m x 2 = $12.8m
9. $12.8.m x 2 = $25.6m
10. $25.6m x 2 = $51.2m ($51,200,000)

In other words, 10x-ing does not add one zero point to your bottom line, it adds three.

Aiming for these kinds of results is important to understand because it is of the nature of the miraculous. It is exponential increase.

You will also live in alignment with your true purpose, a recurring theme of The Nightmares to Miracles Program.

You will undo negative mental patterns, programs, and habits. This is huge. Personally, having been prone to rage and tantrums in earlier stages of my life, as well as alcohol and cigarettes, I know the power of the process that we'll be using to let go of such patterns. Releasing habits that block our being as effective and as efficient as we can be frees us to move forward more powerfully.

It does not matter what you are faced with in terms of patterns and habits that you don't like. All of them can be identified clearly and then undone using the techniques and skills that we will be covering in this program.

You will also deepen a practice to forgive yourself completely for all your mistakes and failures. This is huge because forgiveness of self leads to forgiveness of others. All these things then begin to add up to your ability to manifest your goals more rapidly.

You say, "This is a goal I want to achieve for myself," as you did in the opening questions of this book. By using the many mindset tools outlined in this Nightmares to Miracles Program, you will find that you can set your goals and then manifest the results you desire in faster and more fulfilling and lasting ways.

You will find yourself becoming more successful in all the areas of your life that are significant and important to you. Your entire life will be in divine order. There will be an increased ease in the way you go about your affairs. Frequently you will feel you are in the right place at the right time, which leads to increasing synchronicity. There will be more peace, and more harmony in your relationships. When disruption and conflict occur, you will be better at dealing with them by taking them in stride without falling apart.

You will develop faster learning abilities by using modern technology. In this way, something that might otherwise take years to learn might only take a matter of months, at least in terms of some significant, initial breakthroughs, and we can build on it for a lifetime.

You will learn to crack various codes, or hack various processes, that make life simpler and less stressful. I like the breaking and hacking analogy, whether for health, or financial goals, or relationship goals, because there are sets of codes that you can crack. This is where The 3 Keys to Miracle Success come into play. The Keys unlock doors which ordinarily have security codes that keep us from the knowledge that we need to enter into more high-performance spaces in our lives—these restricting codes can be broken. This is another way of thinking about how to gain access to the skills that we need for greater and faster success.

With these tools and techniques, we can manifest miracles more abundantly in all areas of our lives. As you may recall, the definition of miracles that I'm using here goes like this: miracles are solutions to problems that seem impossible to solve.

So you have a seemingly insurmountable problem or many such problems. Ordinarily there is no way you can see yourself solving the one problem let alone the many problems. To be miracle minded is to allow solutions to emerge for you around a problem that just seems impossible to solve.

I will give, and you can experience, examples of miracles as we progress. In some ways, the more challenging the situation—i.e., the more impossible your problem seems to you to solve—the more significant it is as a test case, to lead you towards being more miracle minded.

As you approach solving problems in this miracle minded way, you will not be the one doing the heavy lifting. You will simply be opening your mind to Higher Power, The Inner Genius, the Divine, or however you choose to refer to this Source of Power within your mind by allowing this Source to do the heavy lifting in, through, and for you.

Finally, through this Nightmares to Miracles Program you will release and heal from your guilt, fear, and anger. Therefore, you will have more energy, vitality, and serenity for all aspects of your life.

I hope at least some of this is of interest to you. Enough to invest just a little time to discover more about this Nightmares to Miracles Program and The 3 Keys to Miracle Success, and to apply the related principles and techniques to your life.

INTRODUCTION

"Miracles enable you to heal the sick and raise the dead because you made sickness and death yourself, and can therefore abolish both.
2 [You] are a miracle, capable of creating in the likeness of your Creator.
*3 Everything else is your own **nightmare,** and does not exist.*
4 Only the creations of light are real."
—A Course in Miracles, T-1.I.24.

Nightmares and miracles are intimately connected. I draw heavily in my work from *A Course in Miracles,* which has had a great influence on my life and become one of my greatest passions. You will find a brief explanation of the course, for those who are not familiar with it, in the section of this chapter "Familiar Frameworks."

A Course in Miracles (ACIM) includes multiple references to nightmares, and the connection between nightmares and miracles.

Indeed, nightmares are a pervasive metaphor in ACIM. When you add up all the references to nightmares, sleeping, and waking, ACIM provides a rich set of clues about its intent to help us wake up from our nightmares and turn them into miracles.

Nightmares are not fun. We can know a lot about a lot of different things, and yet what good is all of that "knowing" if it doesn't rescue us from nightmares that are preventable or fixable or that we can relatively easily wake up from if only we knew how?

That's tragic, isn't it? There is a way for us to wake up from all of our individual (health, wealth, love, and enlightenment) and collective nightmares, and yet we're not waking up because we don't know how, or we're too heavily in the grip of the nightmares, or we think nightmares are all there is.

ACIM provides us with a clear and reliable way to wake up from our nightmares into miracles. The ACIM workbook is, however, a year-long endeavor at minimum, and the rest of the book can be a heavy read.

Here, I lay out some of the best practices in ACIM for escaping our nightmares, and a roadmap for applying these best practices to your own life as a leader, teacher, and coach.

What do I mean by nightmares? We are not simply talking about bad dreams while we are actually sleeping, but about our waking nightmares.

Reversal of fortune, calamity, and disaster beset us all. In your personal life, you may endure bitter relationships, an unhappy marriage, or divorce; you may suffer addictions, tormenting feelings, legal woes, financial woes, relationship woes, and health woes.

In the health arena, nightmares can take the form of horrifying and devastating diagnoses for oneself or a loved one, or some other health tragedy.

In work, nightmares could be in the form of serious loss of momentum, hitting insurmountable roadblocks, toxic relationships and the competition that goes along with them, or never-ending struggles with unrealized potential in yourself or in those around you.

I have been through them all. It seems there's so much information about so many things in life these days, but little knowledge about how we can escape from our nightmares and the associated hardships and traumas that threaten our sanity and peace and safety and security and wellbeing.

Throughout many horrible nightmares in health, wealth, love, and enlightenment, ACIM has been the most powerful method for my own transformation from Nightmares to Miracles. Now, I'm making this system as accessible as possible to you.

Our worst nightmares are usually in the realms of health, wealth, love, or enlightenment, and so we will pay the most attention to these realms of nightmare. Nightmares can lie in the past or the present, or can be things we expect in the future. Whatever the case may be, our purpose here is to use The 3 Keys to Miracle Success to transform our nightmares into miracles.

I have had the basic structure for this book in mind for the better part of a decade but hesitated to bring it to market until I had tested the concepts and practices with a wide enough group of world-class leaders.

My fascination with synchronicity started in December of 1980 amid what I refer to as my spiritual awakening, after which I began experiencing synchronicities on a regular basis.

My fascination with the miraculous started during the years I spent wrestling as a member of a charismatic Christian community. The community was passionate about miracles, about embracing their presence in the Old and New Testaments, and about recreating them in the here and now according to the templates provided in the Bible. One of my main questions as I observed this passion for miracles in the community was, "What is reliable about this approach to miracles, and what is not?"

A parallel concern of this Christian community was the nature of evil. As I prepared for my Ph.D. work to integrate priestly, pastoral, and scholarly dimensions of research and practice in the Episcopal Church, I decided to focus on the problem of evil, with an emphasis on the supernatural dimensions of the problem.

Early on in my Ph.D. program, I realized I would be living with my topic for a long time. As a result, I thought it would be wise to switch to a topic that was more consistently positive. This was how I switched to the dissertation topic of synchronicity and miracles around 1994, two years after I had started the Ph.D. program.

The psychotherapy training program I attended at Blanton-Peale invited me to teach a course on leadership to area pastors. That was how the leadership part of my work officially began.

My mentor in the Episcopal Diocese of Connecticut, Dr. Carol Larco-Murzyn, introduced me to executive coaching.

In my executive coaching work, I work with world class entrepreneurs, leaders, and other movers and shakers. Along the way, I have received enough strong endorsements from these clients to give me the conviction that what I have practiced and refined over the years is ready for a wider audience with some hope of being genuinely useful.

I started my executive coaching and leadership development business, SynchroMind, in 1999. My first dramatic miracle in my business came in 2002.

I was working with a small business in New York City. When I started with this client, they had been in business for 5 years, and had returned a loss on their bottom line each year.

At a practical level, my strategy with the owner of the business was to support stronger functional differentiation within the business. There would be regular weekly meetings of the CEO (the owner) and with the heads of finance, marketing, and operations. Up to that point, there were no regular such team meetings.

Our focus during these meetings was how to increase sales. At one of our meetings, the head of marketing mentioned she had met someone from Oprah's organization at a trade show, and she felt there would be a benefit to continuing contact with her.

In both individual and team coaching sessions from week to week, among many other marketing initiatives, we collaborated on nurturing the conditions in which we might experience a miracle of some kind through Oprah's organization.

One day, while I was at home, I received a call from the head of marketing. She explained she had just received a call from Oprah herself.

She told me she had been unable to contain herself while on the phone with Oprah, and Oprah had to calm her down. Oprah explained to her that one of the company's products would be featured in the holiday issue of *O Magazine.*

Sure enough, when the product was featured in the magazine, sales took off, and the company made a decent profit on its bottom line for the first time in six years. At the time, the business's revenue was around $3 million per year.

Another significant business miracle happened between 2006 and 2012 with an executive who contacted me for executive coaching to find a corporate position.

As we worked on his goals in miracle-minded ways, he found he was also being offered considerable capital to launch his own business. At the same time, we focused significantly and regularly on billionaires as models of leadership in our executive coaching work.

This client began skillfully deploying his access to his billionaire contacts, as well as deploying his team, and his deal-making ability, eventually, to participate in $3 billion worth of private equity real estate deals by 2012. He also garnered media coverage of his deals in *The New York Times, The Wall Street Journal,* the *Chicago Tribune, Crains Chicago,* and *Bloomberg,* among others.

My two experiences in the billionaire zone—the one with Oprah and the one with the $3 billion deal—provided the main impetus for my launching The Billionaire Life, a division of SynchroMind dedicated to leadership in relation to billionaires and synchronicity and miracles.

The Nightmares to Miracles Program, as of this writing, has a coaching component, an online course, and now this book. As with all things, The Nightmares to Miracles Program will continue to develop as I continue to find better ways to present it that facilitate fast learning, and as my own understanding evolves.

Structure of the Book

This book has a number of layers, and outlining them may assist you in following along more effectively. First and foremost is the coaching method. There is a mix of conceptual material and practical exercises throughout to support you in gaining maximum advantage from the time you put into the book.

Also, there are basic themes, concepts, and practices that are repeated in various ways from chapter to chapter. With each repetition, additional nuances and subtle additions are added to the basics. The rationale for all this repetition is to impart a sense of the incessant practice that is needed with these tools so that they take root in the psyche and transform it more and more fully from a nightmare mindset to a miracle mindset. "Practice makes perfect," as the saying goes.

Each chapter of the book also begins with a quotation from *A Course in Miracles* having to do with nightmares. This seems fitting given that the main purpose of the book is to support our fuller awakening from nightmares into miracles.

Also, the book is dotted throughout with miracle stories from my own journey. These miracles are a mix of the personal and the professional and illustrate, I hope, the manner in which various realizations along the way supported my deepening experience of the miraculous. This biographical approach to noting one's miracles will, hopefully, encourage you to document and write about experiences you deem miraculous in your life. Doing this for the miracles and synchronicities in our lives causes them to snowball and to happen more frequently in the service of resolving our most challenging problems and nightmares. There is another reason for my using my stories in this book. This reason has to do with client confidentiality. So it is both intentional that I'm using my own stories and fortuitous that I have my own stories to tell. Occasionally I allude to my clients, but never with explicit identifiers, and only with permission.

Preceding Chapter 1 is a review of some of the conceptual material and practical steps that led me to my current coaching method.

Chapter 1 provides an overview of The 3 Keys to Miracle Success, and how to benefit from using all 3 Keys together.

Chapter 2 provides an overview of The 4 Doors to Miracle Success, and how to use The 3 Keys to be more effective with The 4 Doors.

Chapter 3 describes The Model of the Psyche that I have been evolving for the last 30 years and how this structure mirrors The 3 Keys.

Chapter 4 covers a number of different mind training tools and techniques I have benefitted from on my journey. In most cases I just sort of stumbled on these tools serendipitously, although this might be another way of saying that I was guided to them by Spirit.

Chapter 5 goes into more depth about one of the mind training techniques in particular: the Hawaiian healing method known as Ho'oponopono.

Chapter 6 puts everything we've covered to this point into a format that allows us to easily see all of our most significant goals for The 4 Doors in one place while reminding us to apply the 3 Keys to them at the same time.

Chapter 7 encourages us to take our goals in The 4 Doors, and our applications of The 3 Keys to them, and incorporate all this into a digital vision board (treasure map) for faster and easier manifestation.

Chapter 8 brings the book to a close with some notes about daily practice for commitment and consistency.

CHAPTER 1

THE 3 KEYS TO MIRACLE SUCCESS

*T-1.I.33. Miracles honor you because you are lovable. 2 They dispel illusions about yourself and perceive the light in you. 3 They thus atone for your errors by freeing you from your **nightmares**. 4 By releasing your mind from the imprisonment of your illusions, they restore your sanity.*
—A Course in Miracles, T-T-1.I.33.

The 3 Keys, which form the basis of my coaching method today, have evolved over time, from my pastoral psychotherapy clinical work since 1992 to my Ph.D. dissertation, which I worked on between 1992 and 2003. The 3 Keys also depend on my executive coaching work since 1999. I have been developing The 3 Keys for more than two decades.

In the Ph.D. process, I discerned three theory levels that I was attempting to integrate into my dissertation. These were:

- *The intrapersonal level of theory*—pioneered by Freud, this theory rejects synchronicity (meaningful coincidences) and miracles.
- *The interpersonal level of theory*—this theory is indifferent or neutral to synchronicity and miracles.

- *The transpersonal level of theory*—pioneered by Jung, this theory embraces and accepts synchronicity and miracles.

3 KEYS TO MIRACLE SUCCESS
For Business and Personal Breakthroughs

THE PRACTICAL KEY
• • •

"I set and achieve clear, ambitious, and measurable goals"

"I Go through the 4 DOORS TO MIRACLE SUCCESS"

1. Health
2. Wealth
3. Love
4. Enlightenment

THE BLUEPRINT KEY
• • •

"I am aware of, and undo my negative blueprints"

"I Undo THE MALICIOUS EGO"

> Not Freud's Ego
> Not Jung's Ego
> Ego of ACIM

THE INNER GENIUS KEY
• • •

"I am aware of and use the guidance, strength, and plan of THE INNER GENIUS in what I think, say, and do"

"I Connect with THE SOURCE"

> Of Miracles
> Of Positive Synchronicities

For the sake of brevity, I started referring to these three levels of theory as the *Intra, Inter,* and *Trans* Levels.

I observed that these theoretical orientations also apply to clinical practices and other theory and practice areas, including science, philosophy, and religion. I searched for a method that could integrate all three of these approaches (the Intra, Inter, and Trans Levels) to both theory and practice. But unfortunately, I found that the technical aspects of this method were not accessible or meaningful to others, nor were they effective in helping people trying to solve immediate and urgent life crises. Consequently, I began to focus on transforming this method into something more accessible and useful to others, something that people could apply in their daily lives with ease.

This is how I came up with "The 3 Keys to Miracle Success," in which:

1. The Intra Level became The Blueprint Key
2. The Inter Level became The Practical Key
3. The Trans Levels became The Inner Genius Key

The Practical Key is about getting our worldly tasks done in alliance with other people in the most effective and efficient ways possible. Most people who are focused on this level are agnostic toward synchronicity and miracles. In other words, they appear to be neither hostile toward nor embracing of synchronicity and miracles. They seem neutral or indifferent to them.

The Blueprint Key is about undoing the blockages to being well-adjusted by undoing one's internal conflicts and negative repeating patterns. People who are focused here do not have much patience with synchronicity and miracles, and many reject religions and the supernatural outright, as Freud did.

The Inner Genius Key is about a strong and positive embrace of synchronicity and miracles, as well as the Divine source of these in all aspects of human affairs. The people who are focused here have strong interest in and understanding of synchronicity and miracles.

While people may be focused on one area more than the others, all three of these keys work together to unlock miracles, and it is essential to think of these as working together.

I correlate this model to a three-legged stool. If you want to sit or stand on it to do something functional or practical, you need all three legs. If you only have two legs, the stool will wobble and collapse when you put any weight on it. If you only have one leg of the stool, it will not stand up at all. Similarly, if any of the legs are shorter than the other, the stool will be unbalanced and fall.

We need all three of these working together. We will go into more detail about each of The Keys in just a moment.

Approaching Miracles On 3 Levels

Here's one more brief but crucial sidebar before we go more fully into The 3 Keys. Does talk of miracles and the miraculous make you uncomfortable? Do you think of miracles as the exclusive province of religion? Do you see miracles as relics of a more primitive time and way of thinking? Do you think miracles are a cop-out or the opiate of the masses? Do you think miracles are the way charlatans seduce and bamboozle the gullible and credulous? While there are approaches to miracles that can be indicted on some or all of the above charges, it still remains that there is a TRUTH about miracles and the power they can afford us out of our nightmares. It is this TRUTH about miracles that we are interested in, in spite of all the erroneous or even malicious paths others may have taken in pursuit of miracles. Some may then say there is no one TRUTH but only competing truth claims. This can seem to be so. However, as one pursues TRUTH, it becomes clearer what that is even in the midst of competing truth claims of various kinds.

As already outlined above, we can approach any aspect of our perception by remembering The 3 Keys and their respective correlations. The Inter Level correlates with The Practical Key, The Intra Level correlates with The Blueprint Key, and The Trans Level correlates with The Inner Genius Key. If we consider, for example, three major disciplines that study the human experience—science, psychology, and religion—we can see that how we approach each of them from The Intra, The Inter, or The Trans perspective determines our attitude to the miraculous within each particular discipline.

This array of possibilities is summarized in the following table:

	Science	Psychology	Religion
Intra/ Blueprint	Hostile to miracles	Hostile to miracles	Hostile to miracles
Inter/ Practical	Neutral to miracles	Neutral to miracles	Neutral to miracles
Trans/ Inner Genius	Embraces miracles	Embraces miracles	Embraces miracles

As the table shows, science does not oppose the miraculous per se. You can have scientists who are Intra, Inter, or Trans, and when they are Trans, scientists will embrace miracles. However, when theologians and spiritual seekers are Intra-focused, they will oppose miracles. Some scientists and spiritual seekers will be neutral to miracles, i.e., Inter-focused.

As will be shown later in the section on The Integrated Model of the Psyche, The 3 Keys also correlate with how the human psyche is built. In other words:

1. The Intra Level (The Blueprint Key) correlates mostly with the negative unconscious aspects of the mind, which we can attribute to the *malicious ego*.
2. The Inter Level (The Practical Key) correlates mostly with the part of the psyche (also involving the malicious ego but here in its more conscious or less subconscious aspect), which is concerned with the external field of perception—having to do with the outer world and the people, places, things, and situations in the outer world.
3. The Trans Level (The Inner Genius Key) correlates with the part of the psyche involved in the innermost Divine.

This model of the psyche and the approach to miracles based on it allows us to be exquisitely multilingual. We can approach the relationship between positive and negative aspects within the psyche through either hard science, psychology, or religion. It also helps us to be open to exceptions and differences of opinion based on nomenclature across disciplines. All the while, we are referring essentially to the same things. I say "essentially" because we also want to be mindful of not falling into the fallacy of reductionism, in which we simply collapse these various disciplines and their nomenclatures into one another. We can approach the different disciplines separately and yet discern meaningful correlations between them. This enables us to have a much more holistic understanding of how we are built as humans and how we function. In other words, it gives us an opportunity to look at things from another perspective and does not cause us to look at these complex theories in an overly simplified way. We are able to look at these disciplines, despite their complexities, in a holistic way, and we don't merge all the theories haphazardly but maintain an understanding of their key differences. When it comes to religion, we can be similarly multilingual when considering The Inner Genius concept, approaching it through understandings of God, Christ, Jesus, or Buddha, among many others, while keeping in mind the same cautionary notes about the dangers of reductionism.

The Practical Key

With The Practical Key, the coaching goal is to support clients to get clear as quickly as possible about the goals they want to achieve.

It is interesting to see some clients dance around this when I first ask them what they truly desire to achieve in their professional leadership roles and their personal lives. Sometimes, their hesitancy also arises from not knowing what they truly want.

My main aim at that point is to support them in nailing down a few primary goals with metrics and a timeline, and so I ask the question, "How much, by when, doing what?" This can refer to their personal income, the bottom line for their company or non-profit, their weight-loss program, their love life, and so on.

The Practical Key is defined primarily by this affirmation and the acknowledgment of the following statement, *"I set and achieve clear, ambitious, and measurable goals."* Think of it as a mantra or a slogan.

You will want to internalize this affirmation. Memorize it, and repeat it regularly, starting at the beginning of your day and at periodic intervals throughout the day. A simple exercise like assigning a minute or so to remember and incorporate this affirmation every hour through the day can be quite fruitful. In this way, you are internalizing this affirmation: *"I set and achieve clear, ambitious, and measurable goals."*

This affirmation has several parts. The first section is about the setting of the goals.

One of the things I've recognized over time in my practice is that as helpful as it is to set goals, if we don't also mind-train around achieving the goals, we have many very interesting goals stockpiled but get frustrated about not being able to achieve them.

Over the years, I have learned to combine both setting and achieving goals in a way that works. This might seem obvious to some, but it is not necessarily obvious to everyone. It took some time for me to recognize that for my clients and me, it is crucial to combine deep commitments to both the setting and the achieving of goals. We must allot the same amount of energy to setting the goals as we do to achieving them. This is why the affirmation also includes a part about achieving our goals.

We also want the goals to be clear, ambitious, and measurable, so the affirmation includes a part about this. For instance, let's say you have set a personal goal to lose 20 pounds. Reducing your weight by 20 pounds is a clear target and is measurable. To say you would like to do that in 90 days or six months provides your psyche with metrics, making the whole endeavor more measurable. All this makes it more evident what you are trying to achieve. There is a caveat to time-frames involved in how to set goals. For example, if you assign a month to lose those 20 pounds, your possible inability to do so might make it more challenging to achieve those goals at all and discourage you from your course. I usually encourage my clients to set the goals and the time-frames as they see fit, and then to tweak these metrics to achieve the right balance between what is ambitious and what is also achievable. It may seem complicated, but think of it as taking "baby steps" to complete your goals. Setting measurable goals is the key to increasing confidence, too. Small victories like losing 20 pounds in six months will motivate us to keep going with our other goals. To accomplish our goals, we need to commit to setting and achieving them by making them clear, ambitious, and measurable.

How do we apply this affirmation to The 4 Doors to Miracle Success? (We will look into The 4 Doors in more detail in the next chapter and how The 3 Keys and 4 Doors work together in The Goals Grid and The 1-Page Mind Trainer sections of this book).

For now, it is enough to consider that there are four major areas in life where most of our attention is focused and where most of our blocks occur. Those areas are Health, Wealth, Love, and Enlightenment.

If we have money and love, but we don't have health, life can be unhappy, miserable, or frustrating. Similarly, if we have health, wealth, and love, but not enlightenment, life can become bleak without our even knowing exactly why. In other words, life can become a nightmare of some sort if all four of these are not working well together.

The Nightmares to Miracles Program is about being systematic in tackling each of these areas to make sure that we're optimizing our lives in a balanced and synergized way, and that we're not needlessly struggling with some sort of *nightmare*. The nightmares are our struggles and horrors in life that disturb our peace.

So, continuing with our examples, you set and achieve clear, ambitious, and quantifiable goals in health, such as losing 20 pounds in six months. You set clear, ambitious, and measurable goals in wealth. The wealth goals also include aspects of your career, your profession, and how you make your living. This area also includes how much money you want to make in a year. Say you want to make a million dollars a year, and you want to build up to that over the next three to five years in your business or your profession.

You will set achievable goals concerning your love life and enlightenment as well. You must set target dates by which you want these goals to happen for you, along with a basic plan for how you might go about accomplishing these goals. You want to do the same goal-setting process for yourself in all of the four areas (i.e., in Health, Wealth, Love, and Enlightenment), specifically concerning what you are trying the most to accomplish.

At the beginning of this process, if you are only getting started with internalizing the affirmation, *"I set and achieve clear, ambitious, and measurable goals,"* i.e., the generic version of the affirmation, my recommendation is to do this once every hour through the day, with just a quick 30-second acknowledgment of the affirmation.

Then as you add on more specific and personalized goals for your health, wealth, love, and enlightenment, you can begin to incorporate the hourly practice on your more specific objectives in Health, Wealth, Love, and Enlightenment.

In love, some people want to get out of bad relationships that are causing them nightmares. Some people are lonely and would like to get into relationships or marriages, or have kids. Some people would like to tweak and improve things in their relationships, and so on.

There are all manners of nightmarish relationship scenarios we can find ourselves in. The point is to set a clear, ambitious, and measurable goal for yourself about what you want to see happening in your love life. By when do you want to be in a marriage, or by when do you want to have left a marriage if it is beyond all hope? By when do you want to start having children? How many children do you want to have? Setting the timeline for these sorts of goals will also help in forming them as measurable goals.

Map all of that out. If you are an empty nester, or at a different point of the life cycle of your relationships and parenting and so on, you will set different goals. If you are committed to being single, how do you create a circle of love around you that includes friends, family, professional associates, and so on?

This love area also extends to the love of all life and living things. Humanity at large, philanthropy, nature, the environment, conservation, going green, and things like that are all expressions of love for the world we live in, and things you might set goals on regarding The Practical Key.

The final door to miracle success is Enlightenment. It refers to the ongoing process of spiritual growth by which we become more patient, more loving, more peaceful, more kind, more self-accepting, and more accepting of others. It is also about examining and addressing the effects of our weaknesses and our shortcomings and becoming more resilient about how the negativity of the world impacts our thinking and sense of well-being.

I think it is good to set spiritual goals, such as, "I'm going to read two spiritual classics in the next six months" or "in the next three months," or "I'm going to engage in mindfulness practices," or "I'm going to read ten books on spiritual awakening and growth and development over the next year," or "I'm going to complete the whole of *A Course in Miracles*, which I've been wanting to do but haven't gotten to," or "I'm going to review the whole of *A Course in Miracles* again and so on." Here, we are looking at the commitments we have to our spiritual growth.

Your goals are a way of extending your knowledge of self and your opportunities in life before you miss out on them. You don't have to set all of them just yet at this stage in this book, but it is a good idea to start making a list of them as they occur to you, ready for when we get to the Goals Grid and the 1-Page Mind Training sections of this work.

The Blueprint Key

THE BLUEPRINT KEY: 3 KEYS TO MIRACLE SUCCESS
For Business and Personal Breakthroughs

With The Blueprint Key, my goal is to support clients to address their various traumas starting in childhood. I aim to bring these traumas and painful recurring patterns into clients' awareness, and then also to support clients to begin to clean them off the psychological hard drive in deliberate and consistent ways over time.

In The Blueprint Key, the foundational affirmation that we use is, *"I am aware of and undo my negative blueprints. I am aware of and undo my negative blueprints."*

Blueprints are our toxic negative repeating patterns and programs, negative behaviors, reactions, addictions, and accumulated traumas since childhood. These include all the negative stuff that usually goes unconscious and unnoticed and then affects our experiences at the conscious level. This is how we attract and repeat negative experiences over and over again, i.e., because we have these negative unconscious patterns. Our choices and decisions may appear to change, and yet we may proceed in life with the same underlying negative psychological designs without ever truly realizing their toxicity.

There are positive and negative aspects of our underlying psychological patterns. Here, we are trying to become more aware of the negative patterns or blueprints and then undo them. These negative patterns are a source of great suffering to us. And if not detected as soon as possible, they become more challenging to assess and change. My experience in psychotherapy training and in my practice as a psychotherapist taught me that psychotherapy and psychoanalysis are powerful ways of uncovering our neuroses and of discovering our underlying, unconscious patterns. However, beyond using the talking cure in uncovering these hidden conflicts and bringing them to the surface with a therapist, there is usually not much emphasis on how to undo these negative patterns. I believe much more attention and focus can be applied to understanding and reworking the negative aspects of our psyches.

The overall assumption in the more conventional approach to psychotherapy is that there is no way to really undo our negative patterns and programming. Over time, I have come to think of the psyche as analogous and comparable to the way computers function. You have a delete button on a computer keyboard. You can continuously edit things on the computer by deleting anything you don't like or that doesn't work for you.

I believe the psyche is a lot like a computer in this regard. You can become aware of something that is part of an ongoing negative etching or pattern in your psyche. Furthermore, if you do not like the negative pattern, you can delete it. While it is not precisely true that we can push a delete button in our psyches, with motivation and consistent work on ourselves, we can delete our negative patterns.

The other interesting feature about computers relevant to our discussion of negative psychological blueprints is that you used to be able to use restore points on them. I understand that in Windows 10, the restore points feature has been removed, or at least made less accessible. But previously, if I had glitches on my computer, I could simply restore my computer's operating system to an earlier point, and it would bypass the problem without any deleterious effects. Restore points are better than a factory reset, which removes all the data you've put on your computer. Also, we are only getting rid of the glitches and invasions on our computer by going back to a restore point.

One of the things I had to do to reclaim my computer from some rogue behavior recently was a hard factory reset. I saved all my data and programs and wiped my computer completely clean. Afterwards, it was as though I had a new computer, and I had started over with no contamination or data on the computer whatsoever. It really was not that big a deal to achieve this improvement on my computer. After getting rid of all the data and programs I had put on there, I realized that this cleaning process didn't necessarily have an insurmountable negative impact on my life, as I was simply able to store everything that I would need on an external storage device for future use.

The psychological version of The Nightmares to Miracles Program cleaning process (which is akin to the computer cleaning process described above) can work quickly to clean minor negative patterns. Still, I usually recommend giving oneself about a year to settle into the deeper cleaning process for surfacing and deleting more substantial past traumas.

I've adopted this timeframe of a year for setting the initial foundation of one's deeper cleaning work from *A Course in Miracles,* which includes a workbook. A significant aspect of ACIM is about undoing the malicious ego. The workbook itself takes precisely a year to work through if you don't repeat any of the lessons for more than a day. So, one rule of thumb is to give yourself about a year to really settle into the undoing process. A year of consistent work can change a lot of habits in the psyche.

Now back to the affirmation, *"I am aware of and undo my negative blueprints."* One message contained in the affirmation is a reminder for us to become aware of and keep an inventory of our unconscious dynamics and patterns.

It may seem challenging to do, and you may think, "how can I become aware of my unconscious dynamics?" A relatively quick way to do this is to structure your inventory in decades. For instance, up until you were 10 years old, then from 10 to 20, from 20 to 30, and so on, where you're documenting some of the most miserable experiences you've had in each of those decades, and you're reviewing them.

Just write the headlines down. You can journal more about each entry at another time if you want to, but my recommendation here is to keep track only of a series of quick headlines. Your inventory might include examples such as the following:

- The first day I went to school, I was teased and bullied.
- I was awkward; I didn't fit in and I felt socially isolated,

and so on.

Do this inventorying process for any traumas and other challenging experiences. The purpose is not to wallow in these painful episodes or ruminate on them endlessly. The purpose is to become a bit more aware of the negativity and adverse patterns you want to undo.

Another effective way of getting in touch with our negative blueprints is for us to reflect on our primary caregivers, whether parents, other family members, or other people who cared for us, starting from when we can remember. We then write down how we experienced them negatively. Did they have a drug problem? Were they violent? Abusive? Awkward? Did they embarrass us? Document all those things, and you will have a good sense of some of your negative blueprints. Doing this will begin to help you make specific connections and linkages between your past traumas and your current behaviors and experiences, and to shine more healing light on some of the causes of your negative patterns. How this all works might not be clear all at once, but it will make perfect sense over time.

Another aspect of the blueprint key is the malicious ego. The malicious ego is a sinister, diabolical part of the human psyche. The malicious ego is what we think of as the devil in some religious traditions, although the devil is usually more of an external embodiment of evil, while the malicious ego is a more internal psychological aspect of everyone's psyche. Our purpose now is to take a closer look at how the malicious ego works within the mind.

The malicious ego causes us to bury and forget our accumulated traumas. Have you ever had an epiphany about yourself? Something that becomes clear, and your seemingly blank conscious psychological drive receives an illuminating data packet into it? This data has managed to slip past the repressive ego into awareness. The malicious ego also causes us to use some of the more traditional defenses such as projection. Projection is the process of taking our internalized anger or hurt and attributing it others without being aware that we are attributing aspects of ourselves onto others. For example, if I'm dealing with insecurity, then I might project that insecurity onto others and criticize them as being weak and insecure in some way. I attack in them what I'm unconsciously attacking in myself. Such negative toxic experiences become patterns that get deposited on our psychological hard drives, and then seem, falsely, to be actually sourced in the traumatic and other unpleasant experiences we perceive ourselves as having in the external world.

In Freud's system, "ego" is not a dirty word and does not necessarily represent a malicious factor in the psyche. Rather, it is the aspect of the psyche by which we become more and more optimized over time. The malicious ego we have been discussing here (derived here mainly from ACIM) is not to be equated with Freud's ego. Freud's ego is the psychological vehicle by which we adapt ourselves effectively to the worlds of love and work; it is a measure of how effectively we were managing in life. Jung takes the Freudian concept of the ego and includes a more archetypal, universal, and even spiritual approach to it. encompassing the ego and the psyche as a whole. Furthermore, Jung sees the ego as being somewhat opposed to a spiritual center in the psyche. Freud's system doesn't have a spiritual center in the psyche for the ego to be opposed to.

In Jung's model of the psyche, the ego is at odds with the spiritual center, called "The Self," and The Self is trying to get the ego to open and connect or integrate with it. At the same time, Jung's ego is also not necessarily malicious or sinister.

The ego, as taught in ACIM, is opposed to God or the Divine or higher power, however, you choose to refer to it. This malicious ego is the source of our misery, the source of our nightmares and suffering in life, and in ACIM the goal is not for the Divine and the ego to become integrated but for the ego to be neutralized through the power of the Divine.

Ultimately, we are working to undo this malicious ego, which is the source of our negative patterns and all the suffering we experience within our minds and outside in the perceived world. We are also working to undo the negative programming and the accumulated data that has been generated by this sinister malicious ego. We are deleting all the negative data we have acquired over the years.

Now we are in a position to think of our Blueprint Key work in combination with our Practical Key work. We can combine the affirmations for The Practical and Blueprint Keys much more effectively now as we think of them throughout the day. For instance, one way to approach this combination is through this modified affirmation which now includes Practical and Blueprint elements: *"I am aware of and undo my negative blueprints with regard to my health goals."*

So let's say you have set your goals in relation to The Health Door, and you are using this affirmation to clean out negative patterns about your health so that you can more effectively and speedily achieve your health goals. A negative pattern of yours might be, "People in my family have always been sick," or "Heart disease runs in my family." These are examples of possible negative patterns you've gotten in touch with about your family. Beginning with the combined affirmation mentioned above and using additional tools and techniques that will be provided in subsequent chapters, you can start to clean the negative family pattern out of your psyche. Other common negative patterns could be "not going to the doctors," or "not believing in medicine."

In relation to The Wealth Door, you can use the affirmation, *"I am aware of and undo my negative blueprints with regard to my wealth goals."* Some negative patterns related to wealth might be, "Wealthy people are bad," or "Wealthy people are greedy or selfish," or "I don't have what it takes to be wealthy or successful in my career." These are all negative programming themes we might have picked up. All of them, and any others besides, can be cleaned out through the approach to The Blueprint Key being advocated here.

The same is true with The Love Door of our lives. We might have various kinds of programming in this area that say, "Men are selfish," or "Women are selfish," or "Marriages never work," or "People always leave." We carry this baggage throughout our lives, and it has negative effects on all of our relationships. Whatever the baggage is and whatever the programming is, The Blueprint Key is about undoing all of that.

How we approach The Enlightenment Door is essentially the same. The affirmation *"I am aware of and undo my negative blueprints with regard to my enlightenment goals"* will help remove the blocks and negative patterns regarding our enlightenment goals. Any accumulated baggage we have in regard to The Enlightenment Door, such as, "Religions are all full of charlatans trying to cheat people," or "Spirituality leads to unhappiness in humanity," or "Science is better than religion and spirituality," or "Religion and spirituality are better than science," or any such ideological battles and chasms, can all be set straight over time by cleaning out the negative programs or traumas behind them. The process of removing negative patterns can also be applied to ethnicity, race, and gender, for example.

The Inner Genius Key

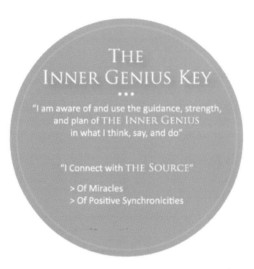

THE INNER GENIUS KEY: 3 KEYS TO MIRACLE SUCCESS
For Business and Personal Breakthroughs

With The Inner Genius Key, my goal is to support clients to describe the ways they approach religion and/or spirituality in terms of The Intra, The Inter, and The Trans Levels discussed earlier. That way, I can customize an approach for them that is attentive to how they are oriented to ultimate questions, and also to the Divine, synchronicity, and the miraculous.

The goal here is to support clients to tap into their inner source of positive synchronicities, miracles, guidance, and flow, regardless of what they call these various elements. These elements of spirituality do not necessarily need to be labeled and can be different for different people. Various limiting spiritual and religious beliefs can also be hidden away in the subconscious without people knowing about them.

Here with regard to The Inner Genius Key the affirmation is, *"I am aware of and use the guidance, strength, and plan of The Inner Genius in what I think, say, and do."*

But what is "The Inner Genius?" This is a phrase that I have chosen to convey this part of my message. I have seen it used in other places, but not in the way I am using it. The Inner Genius, as I like to use it, is a compromise term – a placeholder term. It allows me to avoid engaging in religious terminology and the often interminable debates and controversies that can ensue about differing philosophical and theological camps. It's an easier approach to talking about religion without alienating or offending people.

I define The Inner Genius as "that part of us we all have individually, and in common with one another, that knows the solutions to every problem or nightmare we have." The Inner Genius is something within us that is quite able to do mighty things easily and effortlessly.

A simple way of thinking of The Inner Genius in scientific language is to consider the way the body works. There are billions of chemical reactions going on every second in the body, enzymatic reactions that happen very quickly. These are very complex reactions. They happen all through the body from head to toe, from childhood to old age, and they are vital to keeping the body running efficiently.

We all know this process can break down, and that various bodily systems can sometimes fail. Yes, there can be sickness and serious, catastrophic breakdowns in how all this functions. However, there's also a lot of activity in the body being coordinated between the nervous system, the circulatory system, the skeletal system, the muscular system, and the sensory intake system, and also at the cellular level, and then the billions and billions of chemical, enzymatic reactions that are also going on.

The seemingly effortless coordination of all this complexity on our behalf is akin to the power of The Inner Genius—and that's only from a somewhat narrow biological perspective. The bottom line here is for us to forge a more conscious relationship with our Inner Genius and ask it for help with our goal setting in The Practical Key and the undoing of our negative blueprints in The Blueprint Key. As mentioned before, this is truly a holistic approach. The affirmation The Inner Genius Key summarizes the process of tuning in to The Inner Genius: **"I am aware of and use guidance, strength, and plan of The Inner Genius in what I think, say, and do."**

The miraculous manifestations of our practical goals and the transformations of our negative blueprints are what The Inner Genius is capable of. Like a super amazing chess master, The Inner Genius can manage many billions of calculations for each individual's best path forward, and then also do this for all people together at once at any given moment in time, and then also do this continuously throughout time.

As we practice this Inner Genius affirmation, we become more aware of and use The Inner Genius, but specifically around the guidance of The Inner Genius, the strength of The Inner Genius, and the plan of The Inner Genius in what we think, say, and do. The affirmation is a comprehensive summary of the different dimensions of the relationship we can have with The Inner Genius: **"I am aware of and use the guidance, strength, and plan of The Inner Genius in what I think, say, and do."**

You can use The Inner Genius concept and practice to enhance, profoundly, various microcosm-macrocosm dynamics such as that of the optimal functioning of an individual human body, or the functioning of all bodies at the collective global level, which includes all of humanity.

You can also think of The Inner Genius concept in other scientific ways, such as in quantum physics, where, due to the participant observer effect, the researcher's presence affects the research outcomes. In other words, in broader terms outside of the research lab, you could say that the psycho-neurobiological data you truly possess and process in aggregate in your mind is what you see in your field of perception. In other words, your "inner" psycho-neuro state determines your "outer" quantum field of perception.

I like to stay connected to understandings of quantum physics in all this work in the psyche, especially in light of a powerful dream I had in the 90s. A very loving and genius wisdom figure (like an angelic being), appeared to me and promised to teach me all about quantum physics in that dream. He then gave me illustrations by showing up simultaneously in multiple locations while saying to me that "quantum physics is very easy to understand." In his book, *Becoming Supernatural: How Common People Are Doing the Uncommon*, Joe Dispenza describes in chapter 3, entitled "Tuning into New Potentials in the Quantum," how quantum physics enables us to harness the quantum field – a field of infinite possibilities, to transform obstacles and blockages in our lives.

You can approach The Inner Genius through a second language - psychological language - without resorting that much to the language of science, religion, or spirituality. This psychological language can focus on positive psychology, peak performance, and other approaches too. As an example of psychological language drawn from Jung, you can think of his "Self" (akin to The Inner Genius) at the core of the psyche and the collective unconscious. Jung elaborates on how the Self (Inner Genius) is an overall orchestrating influence for an underlying substrate – the psychoid. This psychoid can in turn be viewed as similar to the quantum field in physics. Ann Ulanov provides an updated treatment of Jung's approach to the psychoid in her book, *The Psychoid, Soul and Psyche: Piercing Space-Time Barriers*.

The third language that you can use to approach The Inner Genius is more explicitly religious or spiritual language. I know people distinguish between those two, and I support those distinctions. Spirituality is the universal experience of a higher power, regardless of form, or what the tradition or organization is teaching about it or facilitating about it. Religious or spiritual language can take many forms, as well. You may be a follower of Jesus, the Buddha, Krishna, Muhammad, or any number of other teachers and enlightened masters who teach in this area of the divine perfection within us, how to connect with it, and how to attain enlightenment. From the perspective of ACIM, there are many ways in which The Inner Genius can show up for us. Here is one example which resonates with the quantum physics approach from science, and that of the psychoid from psychology: "The miracle abolishes the need for lower-order concerns. 2 Since it is an out-of-pattern time interval, the ordinary considerations of time and space do not apply. 3 When you perform a miracle, I will arrange both time and space to adjust to it." T-2.V.A.11(1) Here, we see the Voice in ACIM (akin to The Inner Genius) which speaks on behalf of God, saying that when we commit to being miracle-minded, God can rearrange time and space for us (a very quantum physics idea), so that we do not have to deal with lower order concerns; in other words things become so much easier and flowing for us in the space-time, energy-matter continuum when we commit to being miracle-minded.

To recap, we have explored briefly here at least three different "languages" for understanding The Inner Genius: scientific language, psychological language, and spiritual/religious language. Moreover, there is a conceptual system behind each of these. I like to encourage people to use whatever language makes the most sense to them. I also encourage them to find their own language for this process around The Inner Genius Key or to create a combination of languages and not let any of that sorting and combining impede the essential use of the main affirmation here which is: *"I am aware of and use the guidance, strength, and plan of The Inner Genius in what I think, say and do."* As with our other affirmations, you can remember this one, and use it as much as you need, even every hour of the day if needed.

This powerful source within us—The Inner Genius—is the real antidote to the nightmares we experience in life, and how we can convert these nightmares into miracles.

Now by having a clear sense of where we want to go in terms of The Practical Key, and by undoing some of our negative programming in terms of The Blueprint Key, we are tuning in to what amounts to a metaphor in which The Inner Genius is akin to a *GPS system* within each of us—a loving, compassionate, powerful, caring, and all-knowing GPS system.

The crucial element in all of this is for us to have a relationship, intentionally and consistently, with this inner GPS system; to understand the extent to which it can aid us in every aspect of our lives; and to open up to accept and rely on this magnificent inner GPS system in every area of our lives. If we do not ask The Inner Genius for help in setting and reaching our goals, in undoing our negative blueprints, and in navigating out of our nightmares into miracles, The Inner Genius can't force its way into our lives to help us. We have to let it in. The Inner Genius is also the source of miracles and positive synchronicities we experience that can support, strengthen, and encourage us along our journey in life.

As mentioned earlier, the definition of miracles I am particularly fond of is this: *"Miracles are solutions to problems that seem impossible to solve."* These solutions are derived from The Inner Genius within each of us.

Miracles have their source in The Inner Genius. They come from the power of The Inner Genius working through the mind to disarm the toxic blockages that are causing us to be gripped by various nightmares in the four main areas of Health, Wealth, Love, and Enlightenment.

So now, at the end of our journey with this chapter, we discuss the elements that go into a "miracle mindset." We see that in addition to setting goals in Health, Wealth, Love, and Enlightenment, and achieving those goals from The Practical Key perspective, we are also using The Blueprint Key to undo our negative programming, specifically in these goals. We are also looking to The Inner Genius to navigate us and guide us out of our nightmares and into miracles in each of The 4 Doors to Miracle Success

While The Inner Genius is the main GPS power at work in us, The 3 Keys function together in the manner we are accustomed to with kinds of GPS devices we use in our cars. With The Practical Key, we are establishing where we would like to go, and when we would like to arrive there (destination and arrival time). With The Blueprint

1, clarify + set goals

Key, we are identifying the catastrophes, major obstacles, distractions, and glitches that can impede our progress on the journey (traffic jams, accidents, or under-construction roads). And with The Inner Genius Key, we are tuning into the inner voice that will give us unerring turn-by-turn directions at every step of the journey.

Now for a brief word here about Artificial Intelligence (AI) taking over humanity and all the potential horrors of such outcomes. We can speculate that most people working in AI and machine learning and such other related computer science fields are not that familiar with the in-depth psychological model of the psyche and human mind being presented here. AI and machine learning are two areas of computer science touted loudly and frequently today either as humanity's greatest salvation or humanity's greatest damnation. It appears that that most experts in these and related computer science fields are mostly focused on replicating and improving how the human psyche navigates and performs in the empirical and phenomenal world. It is possible that the malicious ego, in cahoots with AI and the rest, could come up with new life forms that mimic humans in certain ways. And I'm sure AI would be deemed all the more fascinating or terrifying as a result. All this would take us closer to the Hollywood version of "the robot takeover."

A much better use of humanity's obsession with AI and machine learning would be for it to be used to help us become aware of and undo, not overlook, ignore, or power through unconscious blockages, and thereby help us stay more connected to The Inner Genius. This would be a more beneficial use of AI and machine learning instead of their being used solely to try and mimic human functioning and decision-making at its more superficial and flawed physical and empirical levels.

CHAPTER 2

THE 4 DOORS TO MIRACLE SUCCESS

*T-2.I.4. All fear is ultimately reducible to the basic misperception that you have the ability to usurp the power of God. 2 Of course, you neither can nor have been able to do this. 3 Here is the real basis for your escape from fear. 4 The escape is brought about by your acceptance of the Atonement, which enables you to realize that your errors never really occurred. 5 Only after the deep sleep fell upon Adam could he experience **nightmares.***
6 If a light is suddenly turned on while someone is dreaming a fearful dream, he may initially interpret the light itself as part of his dream and be afraid of it. 7 However, when he awakens, the light is correctly perceived as the release from the dream.
—**A Course in Miracles, T-2.I.4.**

The 4 Doors to Miracle Success are Health, Wealth, Love, and Enlightenment. In my life, and the lives of my clients, I have realized that it is possible to spend enormous amounts of effort, time, and resources pursuing learning that will not be beneficial for us when we are facing real problems and troubles in life.

By focusing more of our efforts on these four areas (Health, Wealth, Love, and Enlightenment) in a prophylactic way, we can maintain balance and achieve happiness and success in our lives and all our endeavors. Through this approach, we become more resilient and buoyant in the face of adversity and catastrophe.

The 4 Doors Overview

Another metaphor that helps to illustrate The 4 Doors further is the four wheels of a car. Health is one of the front wheels of this metaphorical car. It is precious beyond measure and irreplaceable. And yet, no one teaches us, and therefore most of us do not learn how to nurture true, deep, and lasting health in mind and body. If the tire is not inspected routinely for low pressure or hindrances, we may end up with a flat tire. And if the health tire is flat, unless we can fix or replace it quickly, that is the end of our journey.

The Nightmares to Miracles Program teaches us how to fix or replace the flat health tire and even prevent its puncture. Or mixing metaphors, the method shows us how to go through The Health Door of Miracle Success consistently and reliably.

When it comes to the wealth tire, the stakes are just as high. There can be no real compelling journey until this tire is in good shape, or fixed or replaced if need be. The Wealth Door will lead you to understand better how to maintain and improve the wealth tire.

When the love tire is flat, no journey can occur because we need four good tires for our car to work. And the love tire must also work for us to stay on our Miracle Success Journey.

When the enlightenment tire is flat, the results are the same—i.e., there is no really effective success journey. This aspect of the journey illuminates the road when it's dark, and we cannot see properly otherwise.

Most of us have four damaged if not flat tires. We are trying to go on this lifelong journey, but our car won't even leave the driveway. We can have a nice car, a good model and make, nice color, and even some fancy bells and whistles, but the four flat tires will not let the car get out of the garage.

Some people only have three flat tires, but bad news—their car won't work fully.

Some people only have two flat tires—their car is still not going to work fully.

Some people only have one flat tire—sorry, their car still won't work fully.

We need all four tires to be working for us to get on the road effectively. It is incredible how many of us are in our cars and not going anywhere very effectively because of problems with one or more of our tires. We want to get going on this beautiful journey of life, but our cars betray us in various ways.

Not to worry. The 4 Doors to Miracle Success are the doors to the auto service center we go through to get each of the tires fixed and in top shape for the long and exciting journey of life.

Pairing each of The 4 Doors to Success with The 3 Keys to Success is the most effective way I know to make a vehicle roadworthy and ready for a trip. This process can be used quickly and effectively to whip a vehicle into shape if it's suffering from debilitating wear and tear.

We turn next to a handful of Nightmares to Miracles examples in my own life, as well as to some examples of *moonshots* (i.e., seemingly impossible-to-reach goals) also in my life, as a way of adding some additional understanding to the material we've already covered.

The Health Door

On Monday, February 17th, 2014, I was admitted to the main hospital's emergency room in Vero Beach, Florida. I had hugely swollen calves, ankles, and feet. I had had difficulty breathing, sleeping, and keeping food down for the previous two weeks, and I had also felt a deep, unshakable inner panic that nothing seemed to alleviate.

I had no idea what was going on. But I suspected that the spiritual and psychological work that I did on myself was surfacing some deeply buried trauma. I figured this trauma was related to several claustrophobic panic attacks I had as a kid and that I needed to work on those more.

Within 24 hours of being in the hospital, I received a diagnosis:

congestive heart failure and arrhythmia. They told me that I would need open-heart surgery to fix a faulty heart valve and correct the arrhythmia.

I was aghast and stunned at this diagnosis. I tried to explain to the cardiologists that there had to be some spiritual and psychological explanation for what was happening to me. That maybe we were missing something, and the answer was in a reevaluation of my spiritual and psychological traumas. I asked if there was a more holistic way to approach this; I was convinced open-heart surgery was too radical, and that something else was called for.

The specialists warned me of the dire consequences of ignoring or delaying the surgery. These included an increasingly malfunctioning heart and premature death if I didn't get the problems fixed. All quite alarming.

As a long-time student and teacher of *A Course in Miracles* (ACIM), I knew deep down what the heart specialists were proposing as the solution to my problem would only be addressing my symptoms. Their solution would work as medicine but not as a cure. I knew the deeper solution involved my applying the principles of ACIM to this health catastrophe so that I could experience a true miracle of healing and a lasting cure.

However, I was getting nowhere with the cardiologists about my spiritual and psychological approach. Despite my opinions and suggestions, they had scheduled my surgery for Friday, February 28th. I doubled down to wage a private campaign to turn things around. I realized with dismay that although I used ACIM regularly in my executive coaching work for team building and conflict resolution, I didn't have a confident idea of how it might apply to such a terrible diagnosis. It seemed like anything I might try using ACIM at that point would be a shot in the dark.

I had my laptop with me in the hospital, and so I started researching online what ACIM teaches about turning such dire medical conditions into miracles. I was convinced there was a way to experience a miracle in this situation if only I could find and apply the right principles – in the right way.

Eventually, my online research led me to Judy Edwards Allen's *The Five Stages of Getting Well*, and I ordered it. When it arrived, I raced through it and learned how Allen had applied principles from ACIM to her terminal cancer diagnosis, and then how eventually she experienced complete remission.

Allen's book helped me zero in on Lesson 136 in ACIM, which says, "*Sickness is a defense against the truth.*" I was grateful for her book's guidance on what ACIM taught her about healing from her *terminal* illness and what I could learn from it. However, it was unnerving to find that in my 20 years of studying and teaching ACIM, I had no real understanding of this pivotal lesson from ACIM. I had no idea how to apply the principles of healing embedded in the lesson in order to experience a miracle and be healed myself.

I worked diligently to understand and apply Lesson 136 to my traumatic experience of congestive heart failure and the impending open-heart surgery, a surgery which was beginning to look inevitable. As I studied all of this in my hospital room, I began to understand, dimly at first, then more clearly, that Lesson 136 and Allen's book were teaching me that I had *chosen* to be sick on a deep subconscious level.

I realized that this sickness was my way of competing with God. I was in a battle of wills against God, and suffering through this pain would be my victory. I learned that this battle was a power struggle between God and me and my pain, and even death would make me triumphant in some twisted way over God.

During one incredibly long contemplative night, during which I wrestled with these emerging understandings, I asked God (as I had done several times before), "Why is this happening to me, and what can I do about it?"

With all my recent study of Allen's book, her experience with her terminal diagnosis, and my accelerated learning about principles of healing from ACIM, I was more open to an answer from God.

The answer I heard that night was that as a teenager, I vowed to willingly be crucified, if need be, to prove my faith in God and as a follower of Jesus. That night, in my conversation with God, I was told this vow was unnecessary, and that I had misunderstood what it means to follow Jesus. I came to understand that my sickness was my distorted way of competing with God and Jesus rather than following them—i.e., I was using my sickness and suffering to hide and disguise my power struggle with God.

God told me that if I gave up my misplaced need to sacrifice myself through crucifixion, I would not be crucified through open-heart surgery. Upon hearing this, I disavowed my earlier years-long dedication to the crucifixion and pledged to follow God and Jesus in truth.

That night, I went to sleep, exhausted by this intense battle to undo my decades-old pledges to suffer. When I woke up a few hours later in the early morning, I collected my urine as usual in a plastic container that the hospital gave me. I had become quite used to this practice as it was standard procedure. To my horror and deep disappointment, my urine that morning was blood red.

Inside, I cried out to God, "How could this be? I've put so much effort into studying ACIM over the last couple of weeks while suffering in this hospital, in order to experience a miracle, and be healed, and this is the result of all my work? I now have a new problem with my kidney that's causing me to pass blood in my urine, in addition to my heart problems? What a nightmare!"

I was frustrated, angry, and scared, and still fuming when the first nurse of the morning came in to check on me. I told her about the blood in my urine, and she passed the news on to the three heart specialists who had been working with me. As each of them came into my room that morning, they voiced concerns over the blood in my urine and then admitted that it would not be feasible to proceed with the surgery because of this development.

It then dawned on me that the blood in my urine was a significant *miracle* in this entire *nightmare*. It was God's physical empirical way of getting the medical experts to stand down from their plans for my surgery, where I had failed to convince them with my psycho-spiritual formulations. My mood changed with the realization that my bleeding kidney was God's best way under the circumstances to block the surgery. The work I had done in rescinding my vows to suffer crucifixion had been honored almost immediately, although in a way that took me a few hours to understand.

I had been scheduled for surgery on Friday, February 28th, but now with my right kidney bleeding, the surgery was suspended. This suspension of the surgery happened just a couple of days before February 28th.

Due to the various complications from congestive heart failure and arrhythmia (such as high heart rate, fluctuating heart rate, vulnerability to blood clots and thus stroke, and also a chance of sudden death from cardiac arrest) being brought under control by medications, I was sent home on Friday, March 7th. The understanding was that the kidney problem would be fixed on an out-patient basis, and then I would return to the hospital for the open heart surgery in several weeks.

I was under the doctor's orders to take things very slowly while at home and avoid going up and down any stairs or doing anything strenuous or stressful. When I had been at my worst with my heart problems, I couldn't even sit upright in a chair in the hospital for more than five minutes without beginning to get dizzy on the way to passing out entirely.

The next phase after I left the hospital was a busy time of seeing various specialists on an out-patient basis to continue preparing for surgery. Meanwhile, I also continued strengthening my new-found understandings of ACIM and miraculous healing.

In a shocking turn of events, I was told on Tuesday, April 4th, that the surgery was no longer needed due to my improving symptoms. The assessment had to be confirmed with an echocardiogram, which, on Wednesday, April 5th, confirmed for the three specialists that I was now no longer at risk.

My heart rhythm and rate had both gone back to normal, and the damaged valve had also gone back to a mostly normal condition. I didn't have any blood coming out of my urine, and my kidney problems were becoming a secondary concern.

After eight weeks off, I started to ease back into my executive coaching work.

As you can imagine, I was truly amazed and delighted by this miraculous turn of events. I am full of joy and gratitude to know that there is a trustworthy and reliable way out of such nightmares into miracles.

The Ego, The Body, and Miracles

ACIM teaches us that *the malicious ego* presides over our lives and is the source of our weaknesses, traumas, and nightmares. As mentioned earlier, this malicious ego is not the same as Freud's ego, or Jung's ego, nor the ego that most people refer to when thinking of everyday conceit, narcissism, arrogance, and self-centeredness. No, the malicious ego is responsible for far more than these issues of personality.

ACIM's ego is a brutal, destructive, sinister, and malicious part of every human mind. It is deceptive and ultimately illusory and makes the holy look unholy, love look fearful, and God look opposable. It is also the source of every collective human trauma such as genocide, the threat of nuclear annihilation, war, poverty, racism, social injustice, mass shootings, terrorism, mental and physical disease, sexism, and every other conceivable malaise of any kind.

The way out of such nightmarish yet illusory individual and collective trauma is through the miraculous healing of the individual and collective negativity embedded deep within the psyche. This negativity has to be washed out of the individual and collective psyche by the Inner Divine Source, The Inner Genius, available to all people.

Miracles are the result of shifts in perception through the power of this Divine Source within us. Changes in perception can solve any problem for us, no matter how seemingly impossible to solve.

The physical space-time, energy-matter continuum our bodies are a part of is an ego-based illusion. The Divine Source is entirely free from this illusion. When we tune into The Divine Source, even for a moment—*A Course in Miracles* calls such a moment a **Holy Instant**—

we also become free from the limits of the body and the physical world in that moment.

We must effectively and vigilantly live in such a way life becomes a continual series of Holy Instants. The process of mental rehearsal and practice by which we achieve our transformation into living from Holy Instant to Holy Instant in a state of limitless release from the constraints of space and time and energy and matter is what ACIM refers to as *mind training.*

Psychotherapists (or any other "helpers" such as coaches, mentors, healers, leaders, etc.) practicing this type of mind training, at their best, are in touch with the Divine Source within. This leads them to moments of freedom from the limiting ego. In this way, such helpers and leaders impart this "freedom from all limits" to those they are helping or leading. I have experienced that it is the actual inner shift of the helper or leader into freedom from their own ego limits and their traumas that helps to liberate the ones being helped, rather than the words the helper or leader speaks.

Anyone in touch with this state of freedom from ego limits and trauma (even for just a moment) becomes an effective healer, helper, or leader. Though they may not be an actual therapist in a conventional sense (they will still need specialized training for that), they have become a liberator of others, a person who helps to set others free, regardless of their professional circumstances. This is akin to the way in which Allen's experience of freedom from ego and body limits as captured in her book about her miraculous healing from cancer helped heal me and set me free miraculously from my heart problems.

Now that we understand The 4 Doors to Miracle Success, the way ACIM helps us to delete the ego and it's negative programming slowly over time, and how we can enter The Health Door, let us now look at The 4 Doors through the "3 Keys" perspective for even fuller understanding of how to become more effective in our personal and professional lives as leaders.

On The Practical Level

First make a list of your health goals, struggles, and known issues. While doing this, think about the healthy habits you want to develop or maintain and the unhealthy ones you want to break free of or change. These could be goals like quitting smoking, taking vitamins, drinking more water, or meditating.

On The Blueprint Level

Next do the following:

- Make an inventory of your most significant repeating negative health patterns.
- Make an inventory of any illnesses, injuries, and poor health issues throughout your life.
- Make a list of all your negative health beliefs or misconceptions you think you might be laboring under.

On The Inner Genius Level

Now look for the hidden benefits of your poor health habits and beliefs. What do you gain from them? What do your "sick notes" excuse you from dealing with or changing? Such seeming benefits could be the release of stress from smoking, or the joy of eating a burger every day. Then make a pact with your Inner Genius that you are done with all the sickness and suffering that you have allowed into your life.

This gives The Inner Genius permission to replace the sickness, negativity, and nightmares with health and well-being. Positive changes will start to happen! In all of this, we are not saying that conventional medical regimens and strategies are not welcome or useful. They are. We are, however, adding The Blueprint Key and The Inner Genius Key to the mostly Practical approaches that conventional medical treatments entail. Also, in all of this we are not attempting in any way to blame or attack people for their illnesses. We are not saying, "You are to blame for your illness." We are saying, "You are responsible to remove any negative programming that may be keeping your health problems in place, and you are also responsible to connect with the Power of the Divine within to expedite your healing."

The Wealth Door

I have worked with and practiced day and night the principles outlined here to get to where I am. I can confidently say that I have escaped the many financial bullets and nightmares of my earlier life. I have worked for and achieved this freedom from nightmares in the Wealth area, in the Health area, in the Love area, and in the Spiritual or Enlightenment area.

In addition to miracle breakthroughs in my own personal finances and wealth, I have worked with entrepreneurs, millionaires, leaders, celebrities, and people from all walks of life on their financial aspirations. Not as a financial advisor, because that is not my area of expertise, but as a coach using The 3 Keys to Miracle Success. As a result of this work, I have assisted clients involved in multi-billion-dollar deals, as well as amazing leaders at the highest levels of government.

Also, I enjoy working with aspiring millionaires and billionaires. I am also deepening and strengthening my effectiveness as a trusted executive coach and advisor to leaders on their multi-million dollar and multi-billion dollar projects. These are but a few of what can be referred to as my moonshots (i.e., my really enormous goals) in the Wealth area. What are your wealth moonshots, your enormous wealth goals? Take a moment to write down your enormous wealth goals in your "Nightmares to Miracles" success journal.

Now let's look more fully at The Wealth Door through the perspective of The 3 Keys to Miracle Success:

On the Tactical Level

Ask yourself the following questions:

- *How much money do I desire to make or have?*

This could be personal income, a one-year goal, or expanding revenue from your business. You could be trying to get up to five figures, six figures, seven figures, eight figures, or ten figures and beyond. Whatever your financial goals are, one of the most important things to do is to write down the **specific** number you desire.

Writing down the date by when you desire to have achieved your money goals is important too. Remember, the affirmation for The Practical Key is, *"I set clear, ambitious and measurable goals."* It is essential to set the date for your money goals to be accomplished. Rather than saying, "I will have X or Y amount of money a year from now, a month from now, or five years from now," which is vague and gives the ego leeway to introduce needless self-sabotaging delays, you want to say, "By April 13, 20xx, I am receiving or making $XXX," and write the specific numbers down.

- *What exactly will I do to acquire my wealth?*

Answering this question enables you to formulate and refine your plans for how you intend to achieve your financial, wealth, career, and professional goals. Are you going to switch careers entirely? Are you going to switch from real estate to medicine? Or are you going to deepen your skills by retraining in various other ways? Do you intend to aim for more leadership opportunities within your specific career track?

In the enterprise area, are you going to add new team members, build a stronger team, or cast a new vision for your team? Also, bigger enterprise goals can be to go from a one-million-dollar business to a ten-million-dollar business or from a ten-million-dollar business to a hundred-million-dollar business. You could take your boutique investment firm from a 50-million-dollar company and begin laying the foundation to get it to a billion-plus dollars. What is your plan to achieve your financial targets? What are you planning to do to achieve your wealth goals?

On The Blueprint Level

- Think about any negative attitudes you might have towards money and wealth.
- Think about your parental figures from childhood and other influential adults. What were their attitudes towards and beliefs about money?
- List the experiences you had with your parents. Were they too casual with money, spending it too freely when there wasn't enough? Or, were they stingy and tight with money even when there was a lot? Was this embarrassing to you? Did their attitudes make things awkward for you? Did they express thoughts such as rich people are greedy, selfish, or bad? Or that making money was wrong in some way? Did they consider poverty a sin or a virtue?

These are all different influences from your parental figures that can have enormous limiting effects on your ability to achieve your wealth goals.

- Were your parents always working so that they never seemed to have enough time to relax with their loved ones? Were they abusive with their wealth? Were they lazy about working and under-achieving? Did you judge them as mediocre regarding money, wealth, and career? Did they earn their wealth ethically?
- What do you feel when you see an affluent person? What do you think when you see someone less privileged? Do you feel guilty about any of this?

- List whatever other negative feelings and thoughts you have had about finances. As a child growing up, did your parents experience financial reversals, whether through the stock market, or loss of employment, or medical catastrophes that impeded their ability to make a living? Whatever the traumas around money, wealth, or career for your parents, write those down.

- Maybe you had friends who were better off than you were, and this was a source of embarrassment and trauma for you. Did this make you feel envious and jealous? Were your financial circumstances better than your other friends'? Were you judged for it? Did you feel guilty about money in any way, either feeling like it was a burden or wanting to help other less fortunate people? Whatever the traumas were, whatever unpleasant experiences you can remember from your childhood, list them.

- As you grew older, what were your financial struggles and pressures? Did not having enough money or not being able to pay your bills make you feel overwhelmed? Do you have a bankruptcy or two in your history? Do you have tax issues and the levies and liens that usually accompany such tax issues?

Continue to list any issues that are part of your financial nightmares—way too much debt, huge credit card bills, loans, having people take advantage of you, steal from you, cheat you, or lie to you. Is divorce a part of the picture, with all of the often attendant financial costs and acrimony? This area can include not being able to keep up with your child support payments. Have you stolen or embezzled money yourself, or have you been wrongfully accused of stealing money.

Whatever your financial nightmares and traumas are, you just have to list them for now. Soon, we will start working on clearing these traumas out of your psyche. But if just listing your various traumas in the money and wealth area makes you feel anxious or even nauseous, spend a few minutes doing some deep breathing. Try and relax. In upcoming sections of the book, we will cover very powerful tools for clearing up such traumatic memories and the negative consequences of these traumatic memories.

On The Inner Genius Level

In addition to the deep breathing, invite your Inner Genius to guide you into healthier attitudes towards wealth. Read, meditate, pray, and ask for guidance from your Inner Genius about which additional methods and practices would be most useful for your situation.

Set an affirmation for yourself such as "I visualize my powerful goal to have 5 million dollars in my retirement account, and to be free from all debt in the next 3 years." Say this affirmation diligently for the next 30 days , saying it as much as possible every day throughout the day. At the same time, set aside periods to do the inner inventory work described above regarding your various financial pain points in your journey thus far.

The Love Door

When it comes to love, let's start with romantic love. In my work with clients, as well as in my own love life, here's what I believe it boils down to:

On The Practical Level

Create a wish list of all you want in a partner and a relationship:

- Make a list of all the necessary qualities you seek in a partner. For instance, they must be loyal, respectful, understanding. Or you can be even more specific and list things such they should have a degree, be this tall or short, etc.
- Also, make a list of any red flags you want to stay vigilant

about. For instance, your partner should not hide things
from you, not be dating other people, not have serious
addictions, etc.
- Finally make a list of all the things that would be deal-
breakers for you, like too much anger, abusive, bad breath,
no ambitions, serious addictions, etc.

Don't hold back from listing things down, be specific and truthful,
and don't lie to yourself about what you want or what you don't want,
as you are only sabotaging yourself if you are less than truthful with
yourself in this exercise.

On The Blueprint Level

- Make an inventory of all your most significant repeating
negative patterns when it comes to romantic love. Think of
all the things you believe you do wrong, your mistakes,
picking the wrong people, or being unable to enjoy life on
your own.
- Make an inventory of your negative experiences with
those who parented you. Think of any traits you got from
them and how their romantic lives made an impression
on you.
- Make an inventory of any other painful and traumatic
experiences you've had with other people about romantic
love.

On The Inner Genius level

Be clear about what *special relationships* are and commit to learning
how to undo in yourself the penchant we all have for special relationships.

As *A Course in Miracles* teaches us, special relationships are relationships based on the malicious ego. Each person in the relationship

seeks in their partner what they believe is lacking in themselves. Essentially, special relationships serve in a myriad of dysfunctional and toxic ways as God substitutes in our lives and in the innermost domains of our psyches. The older more traditional language for these God substitutes is that they are idols. Another way we can think of special relationships is as addictions. Here, our special relationships are not just limited to people but can involve people, places, things, situations, and experiences, as well as chemical dependencies. A special relationship is the overdependence on another person, experience, situation, or thing, rather than on the Divine within us— The Inner Genius.

Thus in a special relationship, when it comes to romantic and intimate partnerships, so long as each person can supply what the other is lacking, there is a deal to continue the relationship. However, when one or the other person no longer feels they can get what they want from the relationship, they will ultimately seek to exit from the relationship. This usually happens with a lot of pain and drama, and then each person usually seeks another person as the next stand-in for The Inner Genius.

Optimal relationships are ones in which each person involved can find what is lacking from The Inner Genius within. When the two people are together, they have a purpose larger than themselves to help the world achieve a similar orientation—i.e., for people in the world to wake up to find the supply for what is needed the most from The inner Genius within.

Intense feelings of attraction and romance are usually a tipoff that one's unresolved conflicts and needs from childhood are being activated. Based on the activation of these unresolved conflicts and needs, the malicious ego attempts to seduce us to enter into a relationship in which we are about to seek fulfillment of our unresolved needs through the other person, an approach that is ultimately doomed.

The Enlightenment Door

I came to Yale in September 1977, thinking I had finally escaped the backward and oppressive meritocracy of the Ghanaian educational system. In boarding school in Ghana, I had experienced squalid conditions, frequent corporal punishment, and a lack of material and technological resources.

At Yale, I had the naïve hope of sitting and studying at the feet of the various reincarnations of Socrates, Plato, and Aristotle, learning, espousing, and practicing with respectability, a blend of Epicurean hippie-like hedonism and antipathy toward oppressive authority. And in my naivete, I also believed I had won a gentleman's sinecure—that I was guaranteed a successful career in medicine, that a life full of wealth and ease would present itself to me as I serenely pursued the nobler aims of the mind and spirit.

Instead, my adolescent beliefs betrayed me when I found that Yale, like Ghana, had intense academic competition and stringent requirements all over again, maybe even more. Besides, I experienced unrequited love, bitterly cold winters, large bursar's bills, racism, and my terrible ineptitudes. I was perplexed and in agony but refused to admit to myself and others that I might be experiencing culture shock and future shock.

I did what I had to do as a biology major to keep my head above water and spent my time and energy in self-pity and misery. I did experience occasional releases from my nightmares during this period such as when one semester, I was very successful in my economics, English, and history classes. In all three of these courses, I felt engaged by the material and saw how the underlying themes in my courses all related to economic and political success. I was well-liked, supported, and encouraged by each of my professors.

In my mind, here, at last, was some good *luck*. Perhaps this should have clued me in that I was better suited for the humanities than the sciences.

Not long after this meaningful convergence in my course work, I experienced a powerful spiritual awakening. which was, looking back, saturated with synchronicity.

When this awakening, this peak experience, occurred, I was exhausted after the first semester of my senior year at college. My mother, my two sisters, and I traveled at Christmas from Ohio to Kentucky to visit some Canadian friends we had known when we lived in Ghana.

During our stay with them in Kentucky, I came upon the books *I'm O.K, You're O.K.*, and *Games People Play*, which were explanations of transactional analysis. I remembered these books from my parents' bookshelves growing up in Ghana, although they did not make much sense to me at the time. I asked to borrow them from our friends in Kentucky. They said I could keep them and, upon our return to Ohio, I started to plow through them.

I remember how easy both books were to read. They made so much sense to me and gave me great comfort regarding my academic and romantic miseries. The books created joy and calm inside me. They positively drove me.

One day, my true spiritual awakening happened while I was lying on the sofa in the living room of my mother's apartment in Columbus, Ohio. I was reading *I'm O.K., You're O.K.*, my mother was in the kitchen preparing us lunch, and my two younger sisters were in their room also reading. Although it was a bitterly cold day in the dead of winter, the sun shone brightly through the living room windows. I was relaxed and excited about the connections and insights piling up as I was reading.

The above collection of synchronicities: my various humanities courses converging in a meaningful way, being together in Kentucky with our friends, and rediscovering books which I remembered from Ghana, all seemed to integrate into a powerful state of awareness that triggered my awakening.

Within a very specific moment in my reading, I realized for the first time that the Christian categories of Father, Son, and Holy Spirit, the psychological categories of Parent, Child, and Adult, from Transactional Analysis, and Freud's Superego, Ego, and Id were all parallel conceptions from different fields.

At that moment, my consciousness began to expand. Time seemed suspended, and my vision seemed directed down the corridors of eternity. I was in a wholly exhilarated state, a state of utter joy, vitality, and insight.

I rushed to my mother in the kitchen and tried to explain what was happening to me. My sisters hurried out of their room to investigate the commotion. Although I could not fully explain my realization to my mother and sisters that day, I was determined to reveal it to them eventually, and to others. It was the most fantastic experience of my life to that point in time.

I realized that day the connection between medical/psychiatric, psychological, spiritual, and supernatural structures in my bones. That awakening was followed by ten years of second-guessing the powerful simplicity of my own experience. I doubted my unitive and transformative crisis, my oceanic experience, because of scientific and religious scruples about "the quest for truth" and positivism. I did not want to mislabel, misunderstand, or misinterpret my conversion through subjective delusions about physical and biochemical epiphenomena in the brain. I wanted to be absolute in my understandings. Therefore, I started assessing this awakening experience from many different so-called objective perspectives.

It was precisely this process of assessing parallels about my awakening experience from various disciplines that started me toward seeing the interconnectedness of synchronicity (from a depth psychological viewpoint) and the miraculous (from a theological perspective). My desire to verify my experience as rigorously as possible eventually moved me away from the sciences after I graduated as a biology major, to becoming a theology student and then a psychology student.

This experience of awakening compelled me to see all of life as interconnected. What I was struggling to do in a restless journey from field to field was clear to me as an effort to unify my fragmented understanding of the relationships between the body, mind, and spirit. I desired to connect things in a way that took both science and religion seriously, through a holistic approach. In my initial commitment to combine these fields through a medical specialty, I described what I was considering pursuing professionally as *"theological neuropsychiatry."* This eventually became modified away from a positivistic scientific approach in favor of an eclectic and more symbolic approach. In turn, this ultimately led me to the Psychiatry and Religion program at Union Theological Seminary and the psychotherapy training program at the Blanton-Peale Graduate Institute, both in New York City.

On The Practical Level

To enter the doors of enlightenment:

- List your spiritual and learning goals.
- List all the questions and curiosities you have about the Divine, and the various pathways for connecting with the Divine you are aware of or interested in.

On The Blueprint Level

- Make an inventory of your doubts and concerns about your faith, spirituality, or life philosophy.
- Make an inventory of your negative experiences around faith, synchronicity, miracles, and various religious traditions and systems of belief you've been affected by.
- Make an inventory of things about the broader world that trouble you.

Think carefully about the unanswered questions you have and the paths you want to explore to answer your questions.

On The Inner Genius Level

Ask your Inner Genius to help you clean out your negative patterns about religion and spirituality and be prepared to listen to the intuitive answers that come up in your mediations and other inner work. A few more thoughts on goal-setting in relation to *A Course in Miracles*. At a very basic level, almost no sensible person is going to argue against planning one's life by setting meaningful goals for oneself, or in relationship to one's leadership, and the related enterprise goals one must set strategically for one's organization. It might therefore come as a surprise to discover in Lesson 135.II.1 of ACIM, the following: "A healed mind does not plan." Just by itself, this sentence might seem to suggest that planning is not something that the mind that has been healed or is being healed by the Divine engages in. However, if we introduce what comes after this sentence from ACIM, we have a much fuller picture:

W-135.II.A healed mind does not plan. 2 It carries out the plans that it receives through listening to wisdom that is not its own. 3 It waits until it has been taught what should be done, and then proceeds to do it. 4 It does not depend upon itself for anything except its adequacy to fulfill the plans assigned to it. 5 It is secure in certainty that obstacles cannot impede its progress to accomplishment of any goal that serves the greater plan established for the good of everyone.

W-135.12.A healed mind is relieved of the belief that it must plan, although it cannot know the outcome which is best, the means by which it is achieved, nor how to recognize the problem that the plan is made to solve. 2 It must misuse the body in its plans until it recognizes this is so. 3 But when it has accepted this as true, then is it healed, and lets the body go.
—A Course in Miracles, W-135.II-12

The rest of the paragraph makes it clear that human planning is so flawed that ultimately the better way to go is to allow for Divine plans to be downloaded into our psyches, which we then execute.

There might be several issues we have with this approach. First, we know, as humans, people have claimed over and over again to be doing things that have been Divinely revealed to them, and that just claiming something has been Divinely revealed does not make it so. There can be mental illness involved; there can be oppression and wickedness involved; there can be demagoguery involved; there can be chicanery and trickery involved. So while the concept might be easy to grasp that it is better to allow the Divine to show us what to execute on, this can be fraught with many difficulties. We looked briefly in the introduction to this book, at how competing truth claims can come into play when we are exploring miracles. Similar issues about competing truth claims can come into play as well when we are exploring what we consider to be impartations of the plans of the Divine to us humans. As with the competing claims that can come into play about miracles, so with the competing claims that can come into play about God's plans for us. As one pursues TRUTH, it becomes more and more clear what that is even in the light of various competing truth claims.

Also, what is one to do until one arrives at that place in one's development where one is safely and accurately receiving Divine plans to execute on? Something has to be done in the meantime, no? So between no planning at all for fear of the ego's hijacking what we do in this regard, and perfect plans given to us from the Divine, we proceed by doing the best we can with our flawed human planning, trusting that eventually we will reach a state of development in which we do truly receive Divine plans to execute on in every area of our lives, personal and professional.

CHAPTER 3

AN INTEGRATED MODEL OF THE PSYCHE

*T-3.VI.4 You are very fearful of everything you have perceived but have refused to accept. 2 You believe that, because you have refused to accept it, you have lost control over it. 3 This is why you see it in **nightmares**, or in pleasant disguises in what seem to be your happier dreams. 4 Nothing that you have refused to accept can be brought into awareness. 5 It is not dangerous in itself, but you have made it seem dangerous to you.*
—A Course in Miracles, T-3.VI.4

Before we go any further, it will be helpful to have a shared understanding of the psyche as well as some basic psychological terms and concepts as they are applied throughout The Nightmares to Miracles Program.

I have been working on my integrated model of the psyche, since the early '90s, layering into it different understandings, refining it, and whittling things away. It represents for me a fairly simple way of looking at the psyche as a whole, while considering the different layers of the psyche involved in our explorations in this book.

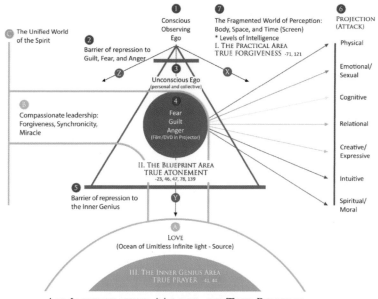

AN INTEGRATED MODEL OF THE PSYCHE

1 The Conscious Observing Ego
2 The Barrier of Repression to Inner Fear, Guilt, and Anger
3 The Unconscious Ego (Personal and Collective)
4 Fear, Guilt, and Anger (Film)
5 The Barrier of Repression to the Inner Genius
6 Projection (Attack)
7 The Fragmented World of Perception: Body, Space, and Time,
Levels of Intelligence (Screen)

A Love
B Compassionate Leadership
C The Unified World of the Spirit

I The Practical Area – True Forgiveness
II The Blueprint Area – True Atonement
III The Inner Genius Area – True Prayer

The Conscious Observing Ego

The topmost part of the psyche, the conscious mind, that we are all aware of sits at the top of the triangle in the diagram. This conscious observing ego, through which most of us know ourselves, observes what is on the right-hand side of the diagram in the direction of X: what we can refer to as "the screen of perception," as in a movie screen (#6). The conscious observing ego is watching external reality as if a movie were playing on a screen. We interpret this external reality as physical, emotional, sexual, cognitive, relational, creative, expressive, intuitive, and spiritual and moral things going on in our field of perception. Some people know these various categories as related to the chakras.

The Barrier of Repression to Inner Fear, Guilt, and Anger

As you go down the diagram, you go into deeper, less conscious, or more subconscious or unconscious layers of the mind. The next number in the sequence here is number 2 where you have what can be referred to as a "barrier of repression" to inner fear, guilt, and anger. That is the horizontal line (#2) in the diagram. This barrier is like a gate that is kept tightly locked by the defenses of the ego so that, under normal circumstances, we do not have access to the area designated as #3 (the personal and collective unconscious ego). This barrier also stops entrance to the area designated as #4—i.e., the enormous repository of fear, guilt, and anger that is buried deep in this unconscious region of the psyche.

There is a lot of intense psychological theory and practice around all of this, but we are mainly hovering around the pioneering work of Freud when we look at the areas designated as #1, #2, and the topmost part of #3 in the diagram.

The Unconscious Ego (The Personal and Collective)

As we descend deeper downwards into this diagram of The Integrated Model of the Psyche, we are moving more into the realm of Jung's pioneering work on the psyche. Jung brings in a better understanding of the collective unconscious, which has to do with the archetypes that connect all of us.

He also has what he referred to as a "divine" component of the psyche known as "the Self", with a capital S to distinguish it from "the little self" of the ego of an individual person or of humanity collectively. So this Self can be thought of as the divine Center in Jung's model of the psyche which all humans have in common, although it is buried deep in the unconscious mind. Freud does not have a divine element in his model of the psyche. Freud also does not have a well-developed sense of the collective unconscious. His treatments of Eros (the life instinct), and Thanatos (the death instinct), the Oedipal drama, and the societal expectations derived from the superego, although, can all be seen as very rudimentary parallels to what Jung would later develop more elaborately as the universal archetypes that we all share deep within the psyche.

What is most important here for our focus on developing miracle mindsets is that we all have this barrier of repression. Underneath it, we have all these unconscious elements of the personal and the collective ego, which include a huge accumulation of toxic fear, guilt, and anger.

A Course in Miracles teaches that the external physical world that we perceive is the result of our projections of this buried fear, guilt, and anger into the field of perception. So, it is a little bit like the way a film is the source or the basis of the images on the movie screen which originate in a projector. This film gets projected onto the screen in a movie theater. So just as in a movie theater, what we are essentially experiencing in our lives as external reality are various images projected onto the screen of our awareness from our unconscious fear, guilt, and anger. This idea is also similar in some ways to Plato's Allegory of the Cave, in which people are in a cave and they are observing certain fantastic images that appear on the wall of the cave. In truth, of course, the images that they are seeing are really their own shadows being projected onto the wall of the cave. The reality or the Truth lies behind them while they behold projections of their own shadows in front of them.

Fear, Guilt, and Anger (the Film)

Now let's take a look at the fear, guilt, and anger referred to by #4 in the diagram. A lot of the mind training techniques that will be described in the upcoming pages, as well what *A Course in Miracles* teaches, are all designed to dissolve fear, guilt, and anger, as well as the malicious ego itself, which gives rise to the fear, guilt, and anger in the first place. This ego-generated fear, guilt, and anger is what turns into the nightmares that we experience in our lives.

Unfortunately, many people are seeing the images that are being projected into the field of perception from the accumulated yet unconscious fear, guilt, and anger within. They are attempting to manipulate the external images in order to change and improve what they are experiencing in life; engaging in this external manipulation of our images does no good in a lasting way. By manipulating the images we see on the screen of the field of perception, i.e., by trying to influence the people, places, things, and situations in our field of perception, we hope to make the movie we are projecting into a better one. This is as futile in the long run as trying to change the outcome in a movie we might be watching on TV or in a movie theater by yelling at the characters on the screen.

What *A Course in Miracles* is trying to awaken us to is that yelling at the screen (our projections) in life is not going to change anything about them that effectively. The place to engage in real change in what we perceive is by cleaning up the fear, guilt, and anger in area of our psyches represented in #4 in the diagram. This is the area of our psyches where we can delete, clean, or remove and replace our accumulated toxicity, and thereby replace what's in there with a better film or DVD, and thereby experience a better external movie.

The Barrier of Repression to the Inner Genius

Perhaps now a question on your mind is *how do we clean up and delete the accumulated toxicity that resides deep in our psyches?* Here's the answer: we clean up and delete our accumulated inner toxicity by using the conscious mind to connect with the ultimate Divine source within our psyches, i.e., the region designated as #5 in the diagram.

This inner source of goodness—what I refer to as The Inner Genius—is an ocean of limitless, infinite light, love, and power, and any of the other verities that we can think of. When we connect intentionally with this Inner Genius, we unleash positive healing forces and powers that can, over time, clean up and delete all of our inner accumulated toxicity. As we will see further on in the book, this process of connecting with The Inner Genius, the Divine love within, of drilling down into it, is what *A Course in Miracles* refers to as "mind training." It is what many meditation and prayer disciplines and other mental conditioning approaches are all about. Learning to connect in this way with The Inner Genius is one of the most crucial aspects of developing a miracle mindset.

When we refer to our diagram, we can see that area #6 refers to the movie of life that we are living in, including the various nightmares that we are stuck in. We are asleep to the unconscious guilt, fear, and anger that are causing the nightmares in our external movies. We are also asleep to The Inner Genius, which can awaken us from our nightmares by cleaning out our accumulated toxicity. By drilling down into the Divine within, we permit the unleashing of Divine power into the part of our psyches that contains our accumulated guilt, fear, and anger. We permit this Divine power to clean out the fear, guilt, and anger that are showing up as our nightmares in life.

However, drilling down and connecting with the Divine within, The Inner Genius, is easier said than done. This is because of the second barrier of repression in the psyche designated in the diagram by item #5.

So we see that not only is the malicious ego blocking us (#2) from becoming aware that our nightmare movies (#6) are the result of our accumulated inner toxicity (#4), and the projection of this toxicity into our fields of perception, but the malicious ego also does not want us to become aware of or connect effectively with the antidote (The Inner Genius) to this negative material we've accumulated in our psyches. The malicious ego seeks to block our connection with the Inner Divine love, the medicine that heals our accumulated toxicity.

A lot of the spiritual and psychological work (whether through *A Course in Miracles* or other paths and techniques), that we aim to do, is at its best, about undoing these barriers of repression in ways that we can handle safely so that we do not get engulfed and overwhelmed by our inner toxicity on the one hand. On the other hand, various spiritual best practices are also designed for us so that we do not get flooded by the inner Divine light in ways that are frightening and overwhelming to us either.

In other words, if these barriers of repression are not undone gradually and safely, both types of undoing (of the first and second barrier to repression) can be mind-blowing in unpleasant ways. Too much awareness of our inner toxicity too quickly can be detrimental to us; too much cleaning and healing light released into the psyche can also be detrimental to us. So, while the barriers of repression are obstacles to uncovering what is buried and then healing it through inner Divine love, we have to be careful in how we go about opening up these barriers; otherwise, we could be in for some unpleasant experiences.

Projection (Attack)

Here's a summary of the main points we've covered thus far about The Integrated Model of the Psyche. If one can change the film that's in the projector (#4), one goes from projecting a horror movie or a nightmare (#6) to having a happy, peaceful, loving, joyful, and happy movie (#B), which is the purpose of connecting with our inner Divine power (#A and #III).

The 3 Keys to Miracle Success being advanced in this book are based on understanding this premise: the world we see with our physical eyes, and all the issues and problems presented to us through the physical world, including the experiences we have in our bodies, as well as our experiences with the bodies of all other people, is like a movie we are projecting from deep within our minds. The implication of this premise is that the true solution for every problem and issue we have lies at the level of the movie we are projecting from within our minds. In other words, change the inner movie, eliminate the problem.

The Fragmented World of Perception: Body, Space, and Time; Levels of Intelligence (The Screen)

Another aspect of the world that we see "out there" in the field of perception—in the nightmare world that we think is actually the real world—is that it's a fragmented world of perception. There is the body, and space, and time, and matter, and energy, and also there are the various levels of intelligence. In other words, the field of perception contains a terribly fragmented world of duality.

This whole fragmented and dualistic world (#7) is what we think of as reality when we're metaphorically asleep within our ego projections, just as when we're actually sleeping, and we have a nightmare, we experience the nightmare as grippingly real until we wake up and realize that we were just having a bad dream. Similarly, the physical material world we appear to be living in, with all of its tragedies and suffering, is just like a bad dream and nightmare. It appears all too real to us until we're awakened from it by the inner Divine.

A: Love

In the diagram of The Integrated Model of the Psyche #A depicts the ocean of infinite universal love that is available to us. To have a very rough sense of the scale involved, imagine that the observing ego (#1) in our diagram is the size of a single human being. Now, imagine that the rest of the ego (#2, 3, 4, and 5) would all then combine to be about the size of a large cruise ship on the ocean. The rest of the psyche that makes up the inner Divine love and light would then be the entire ocean on which this cruise ship is floating. So, in relative terms, the ego and all its nightmarish shenanigans can seem quite overwhelming, but when we shift to a better understanding of how vast the ocean of love and light is, only then do we realize that inner Divine love is much more vast and significant than the ego. Moreover, with some training on how to do so, we can permit the inner Divine to help us overcome the puny ego through love.

B: Compassionate Leadership

All of these aspects of The Integrated Model of the Psyche that we've covered so far can be added to a leader's tool-kit as part of the miracle mindset. When this is done, there is an ever-increasing sense of being in a state of flow, with the right people, places, things, and circumstances showing up at the right time and in the right way for enhanced effectiveness in one's leadership projects, as well as for a greater sense of fulfillment and peace as one goes about one's projects.

One major hallmark of this type of leadership, in which the leader is upgrading their psyche to a miracle mindset and transforming nightmares into miracles, is a richly enhanced ability to support and even coach one's direct reports, supervisees, and even other C-suite team members to be more miracle-minded. A key ingredient of such miracle-minded leadership is a sharp decrease in tyrannical, oppressive, bullying, and even abusive behavior. This is because the miracle-minded leader now understands that positive, lasting individual and organizational change does not come about by trying to coerce, force, and push around the unproductive, dysfunctional, and destructive people, places, things, and situations in one's leadership movie. No, not at all; the far more productive approach is for everyone's transformation from the inside out, following the principles and methods being laid out here.

This translates into miracle-minded leaders, who then in turn coach others to embark on similar miracle-minded approaches to leadership development from the inside out, giving rise to virtuous circles of teamwork and productivity within various corporate divisions and cultures.

C: The Unified World of the Spirit

Over time, The Integrated Model of the Psyche helps to train us to ask ourselves, in both our leadership work and in our personal lives, "Do I want the fragmented nightmarish world of the ego, or do I want the peaceful, miraculous world of The Inner Genius?" This question usually leads, in turn, to the obvious response of, "Well, of course, I prefer the peaceful, productive, miraculous and unified world of the Inner Genius, rather than the destructive, nightmarish, conflicted, and catastrophic world of the ego."

This leads increasingly to an ability to switch channels on the TV of our minds from the ego channel to The Inner Genius channel—to switch out the nightmarish horror-filled DVD in our mental DVD player to a happy movie which is inspiring, rewarding, and fulfilling to watch and participate in.

So, there you have a quick overview of what I call The Integrated Model of the Psyche, which I have been developing for the better part of two decades. We will now turn briefly to how all of this relates to The Practical Key, The Blueprint Key, and The Inner Genius key. Even more importantly, we will see how we can learn and practice how to switch from the ego/nightmare channel to The Inner Genius/miracle channel more and more quickly and expertly in our business lives as well as our personal lives.

I: The Practical Area – True Forgiveness

The Practical Area is concerned with the everyday world, which is, in some ways, the nightmare world that is out there where we are trying to make a living and relate to other people and so on. This field of perception is what I refer to as "the practical area of life." This area is where we apply our Practical Key affirmation: "I set and achieve clear, ambitious, and measurable goals," which you will remember from earlier in the book.

From the perspective of ACIM, the reason why we associate the practical outer world of perception with True Forgiveness is because we are in dire need of letting go of our dysfunctional attachments and even addictions to what we "see" in our fields of perception. The grievances we have towards the various people, places, things, and circumstances in our practical fields of perception involving the outer world result from us projecting outward our inner toxicity.

Thus, in True Forgiveness, we come to realize that what we're aggrieved by in our fields of perception are a series of bizarre nightmares that the ego has conjured up to distract us. We're simply going to let these nightmares go by, waking up from them with the help of the power of The Inner Genius. We wake up to a realization that our nightmares have no ultimate reality, and therefore we can let them go.

This is a very different approach to forgiveness than saying to someone with whom we are upset, "You've upset me and hurt me deeply, but I'm going to let you off the hook about it all." This may well be a type of forgiveness, but it is not what ACIM refers to as True Forgiveness.

II: The Blueprint Area—True Atonement

The Blueprint Area is this buried toxicity that we're trying to clean up. From the perspective of ACIM, the reason we associate The Blueprint Area of inner toxicity with True Atonement is because we are trying to clean up or correct or undo our inner fear, guilt, and anger. It is such negative residue and programming that give rise to our nightmares in the so-called outer world. This undoing of the accumulated inner toxicity and error is what ACIM refers to in part as Atonement. I refer to it as True Atonement; to distinguish it from other forms of atonement that are more about exacting a price or sacrifice for our misdeeds than simply deleting our mistakes and errors, as ACIM teaches that (True) Atonement does.

In fact, Atonement is so significant in ACIM that it says the following about it:

5. The sole responsibility of the miracle worker is to accept the Atonement for [themselves]. 2 This means you recognize that mind is the only creative level, and that its errors are healed by the Atonement. 3 Once you accept this, your mind can only heal. 4 By denying your mind any destructive potential and reinstating its purely constructive powers, you place yourself in a position to undo the level confusion of others. 5 The message you then give to them is the truth that their minds are similarly constructive, and their miscreations cannot hurt them. 6 By affirming this you release the mind from overevaluating its own learning device, and restore the mind to its true position as the learner
—**A Course in Miracles, T-2.V.5**

In other words, the central task, focus, or preoccupation of any would-be miracle-worker is to accept Atonement for themselves. All miracle work begins and ends with atonement.

III: The Inner Genius Area – True Prayer

The Inner Genius Area is the Divine treasure house, even more deeply buried in the psyche, where all healing emanates from. From the perspective of ACIM, the reason we associate The Inner Genius with True Prayer is because this is where we connect with our true source of power within. It is called True Prayer because it represents a powerful unbreakable connection to our source; it is not about asking for things or for help per se (as in ordinary prayer) but is concerned with our being constantly connected to our true inner power source.

As should be evident by now, the 3 Keys to Miracle Success (The Practical Key, The Blueprint Key, and The Inner Genius Key), are derived from the understandings of these 3 main areas or "structures" of the psyche, i.e., The Practical Area, The Blueprint Area, and The

Inner Genius Area. I have found that it is enormously helpful to know that The Nightmares-to-Miracles Program is based on some of our best current understandings of how the psyche is structured and built, and therefore of how it functions in its various parts and also as a whole.

Here are a few more points about The Integrated Model of the Psyche:

1. One of the most important things we can learn to do and practice continuously in our lives and leadership is how to switch channels from the ego-nightmare channel to The Inner Genius-miracle channel. We also want to upgrade the metaphorical software that our minds are being run on. Or even more accurately, we want to activate more and more powerful latent functionalities that are already a part of our psyches but that we are largely unaware of.

So, for instance, let's say that we are aware that practicing in an ongoing way how to switch channels from the ego-nightmare channel to The Inner Genius-miracle channel is a good idea, and yet we're missing the idea that a huge part of this process being effective is to understand how to delete the toxic material on our psychological and spiritual hard drives. This can lead to massive ineffectiveness. We do have powerful deleting technology built into our psyches, so we need to learn about these latent functionalities and activate them. There are other similar and powerful latent functionalities within the psyche that can be activated as part of one's miracle mindset. We will touch on some of these in the upcoming pages of this book.

2. The various elements of The Integrated Model of the Psyche are akin to an operating system. This operating system can be upgraded constantly from within if we know how to do it.

3. We can then run various ever-improving applications on this operating system.

4. AI and deep learning, and other emerging innovations in computer science and digital technologies are actually themselves projections from humanity's individual and collective psyches. Some

of these innovations are the projections of the ego-nightmare channel, and some are extensions of The Inner Genius-miracle channel.

Most people pioneering the innovations in these fields are unaware of this distinction, and so they are not intentionally innovating with The Inner Genius rather than the ego , so we are going to keep getting mixed results. We'll be much better off if our innovating, in this field and others, is based on an accurate rather than faulty understandings of how the psyche is structured and how it functions. One key test of whether these technologies are being innovated from the ego or The Inner Genius is whether they enhance The Inner Genius abilities we all already have, or whether they are competing with The Inner Genius in trying to re-create and replicate human beings and human intelligence. This ego-based aspiration is a very different project than using such tools as AI to enhance our already-given Inner Genius abilities.

CHAPTER 4

MIND TRAINING

*T-6.V.2. How can you wake children in a more kindly way than by a gentle Voice that will not frighten them, but will merely remind them that the night is over and the light has come? 2 You do not inform them that the **nightmares** that frightened them so badly are not real, because children believe in magic. 3 You merely reassure them that they are safe [now.] 4 Then you train them to recognize the difference between sleeping and waking, so they will understand they need not be afraid of dreams. 5 And so when bad dreams come, they will themselves call on the light to dispel them.*
—A Course in Miracles, T-6.V.2

Mind training is my favorite phrase for describing how we go about learning how to switch our minds from the nightmare-horror movie ego channel to the miracle-happy movie Inner Genius channel. I learned about the phrase "mind training" originally from ACIM. Mind training can be described simply as embedding different positive phrases, messages, and programming into the mind to alter the mind in a positive, favorable direction. Going beyond ACIM and how it uses the term, there is a wide variety of approaches to mind training. Here are some of the methods I use personally and with clients, as well as some that I think it's a good idea to be aware of even though I haven't used them or don't currently use them myself.

Affirmations

Affirmations are the basis of mind training and self-improvement. They are brief phrases, in the present tense using positive language, repeated often as chants or mantras, prayers, songs, hymns, and the like, and designed to focus the mind on desired behaviors by transforming challenging problems, behaviors, and beliefs.

As you know by now, each of The 3 Keys in this Nightmares to Miracles program has its own foundational attendant affirmation:

- For The Practical Key, this is the foundational affirmation: *"I set and achieve clear, ambitious, and measurable goals."*
- For The Blueprint Key, this is the foundational affirmation: *"I am aware of and undo my negative blueprints."*
- For The Inner Genius Key, this is the foundational affirmation: *"I am aware of and use the guidance, strength, and plan of The Inner Genius in what I think, say, and do."*

You can make your own affirmations for anything that feels significant to you that you want to pursue.

Affirmations are said in the present tense, so you say, for example, "I set and achieve...," rather than, "I will set, and I will achieve..." Many people believe using the future tense defers the intention, forever placing the desirable behavior in the future and unconsciously sabotaging the intention.

Similarly, affirmations focus on the desired replacement behavior rather than the undesirable behavior. If you say, "I don't smoke," the image conjured up is of you smoking, again defeating the intention. Instead, say, "I am free from smoking," where the emphasis is now on the essential freedom from the limiting behavior or mindset.

Affirmations are most effective when they are clear, direct, and appeal to your true Inner Genius's vision of yourself. The stronger and more passionately you feel about the affirmations, the more effective they will be. If you find yourself inwardly contradicting your affirmations, add "I choose to believe" to the beginning to reduce the internal friction. Otherwise, you are in danger of unintentionally reinforcing the negative belief with your passionate adherence to it every time you half-heartedly chant a weak affirmation. If you cannot get on board with an affirmation as it is presented to you, it is better to tweak it until you can accept and believe it in stages.

Guided Imagery and Visualizations

Guided imagery and visualizations often consist of an audio program in which someone is leading you through a series of desirable images. After a brief introduction, in which you may be encouraged to meditate or sit comfortably, the narrator will use descriptive language to paint images of, say, idyllic settings and suggest you imagine a series of symbolic acts. For example, you may walk beside a beautiful river, walk across a bridge, and on the other side, be led to a spot where you dig for beautiful, buried treasure, which represents the new and desired results. There are endless iterations of these types of guided meditations that can be used to improve one's health, finances, and relationships.

(See the appendices for suggested resources on all of the mind training techniques discussed here).

Vision Boards

Vision boards can be physical or virtual, and they contain images and text designed to inspire you to reach your goals and live your best life.

Physical vision boards can be of corkboard, cardboard, or even designated wall space, where we put pictures cut out from magazines and little snippets of inspirational words and affirmations pasted into a collage. Put the vision board up somewhere and look at it, relate to it, and connect with it regularly. The intention is to manifest into our lives the things we put on our vision boards.

There are also electronic versions of vision boards. One particular approach that I am partial to is using PowerPoint slides and decks to make my vision boards. You'll discover much more about the approach I use in this regard in the chapter on The 1-Page Mind Trainer.

Hypnosis Programs

Hypnosis programs usually have three parts to them. The first part is an induction, which counts down the surface mind to quieter and quieter levels of awareness. The second phase supplies many affirmations or other positive messages for the mind to absorb and be transformed by, which end up being deeply embedded in the mind. The third phase is usually a count up, which wakes you up from the hypnosis process.

I am a fan of hypnosis programs due to my personal success with them. At one point in my doctoral program in the 90s, I ran into a horrifying block. I could not pass my German translation exam. I tried everything I knew to try at the time. I had a tutor, I was in a class, and I was studying German as much as I could, but nothing was helping me. I even thought of relocating to Germany for six months or even a year in order to absorb the language more organically, almost like you do as a kid when you're growing up. I was desperate to find a solution to my repeated failing of this two-hour test.

Then one day, I stumbled on a hypnosis audio program in cassette-tape form in a store, bought the program, and started using it. This hypnosis program made all the difference in the world for me. It helped me finally pass my German exam. Now, I did have to listen to it, over and over again, and I followed the instructions it gave me. Then it really helped repair a part of me that was blocking me from passing this exam.

Since then, I have used and advocated hypnosis programs for just about anything it is we desire to improve or achieve in our lives. For anything that I am trying to break through on, or anything a family member or a client is trying to break through on, and for anybody who will listen to me on this topic, I advise the use of hypnosis programs. For just about every area of your life where you are trying to make a breakthrough, there is a hypnosis program that could help, and they come in all sorts of updated technologies now, such as MP3s.

Subliminals & Triliminals

Subliminals and triliminals are messages embedded most often in audio programs, but sometimes in video programs too. Subliminal messages flash across the mind in rapid-fire ways so that the mind does not pick up or resist the individual phrases but instead absorbs the overall message.

Audio subliminals are typically listened to with headphones. While listening, you can be watching your own 1-Page Mind Trainer (to be discussed later) or doing other things such as reading articles, catching up on emails, or even watching movies. You can have the subliminal audio playing in the background, and you don't have to be watching anything directly related to the subliminal message itself.

Video subliminals have a visual component in addition to the audio. The video versions tend to be shorter, usually not longer than ten minutes, and you receive the audio programming through two channels (left and right) of your headphones.

Much like affirmations and hypnosis programs, there are subliminal tracks available to help you improve almost any area of your life you might be struggling with, from health and wealth to relationships and spirituality.

If you have difficulty finding subliminal audio or video programs that represent your ideal desired outcomes, there are even apps now that enable you to turn your affirmations into subliminal audios and videos of your own.

Triliminals include three different audio layers such that one set of messages is beamed to the left ear, then a different set along the same theme is beamed to the right ear, while yet a third set of messages is delivered in stereo and heard in the center of the mind between the left and right ears. You must listen in stereo with headphones for triliminal tracks to be effective, and it is usually there are three distinct places where messages are being offered up to the psyche. Please note that none of these tools and practices are substitutes for competent professional medical and/or psychological help.

Meditation

Mediation usually focuses on regulated breathing and progressive relaxation of the body. Many guided imagery recordings open with an introduction encouraging listeners to meditate while listening to the program. The basic essence of meditation is to quiet the busyness of the mind. There are many ways of doing this, but breathing is one of the more common forms of tuning in to a quieter part of the mind and settling down.

Mindfulness

Mindfulness is using meditational awareness but applying it in daily life to whatever we are doing, be it driving, eating, cooking, or exercising. No matter what we're doing, we practice doing it with a meditational or meditative quality in which we are as fully present in the moment as possible and not wandering off permanently into other thoughts about other things we could be doing. This involves the art of being present and giving our full attention to everything that we do in the moment.

A Course in Miracles

A Course in Miracles was my introduction to mind training. ACIM distinguishes mind training from its opposite, which it refers to as mind wandering. Mind wandering is where the mind is captivated by the ego, which is mostly malicious in intent, and wants to distract us, get us to meander endlessly and to suffer fear, guilt, and anger, and do hurtful things to ourselves and other people. Mind wandering occurs in the illusory nightmarish realm that ACIM aims to wake us up from. So, mind training is the process of waking from the nightmare that the ego wants to keep us stuck in.

ACIM has 365 workbook lessons, one for each day of the year. And these give us a great workout in mind training. Each exercise trains us in a specific way to relinquish the ego and its contents in our minds.

There are also over 700 additional pages of theoretical text and material, together with material on prayer and psychotherapy vital to any student of ACIM. I find that listening to the text on audio, through an audiobook, over and over again is a great way to enhance the mind training process ACIM teaches. Using the audio version of ACIM, I find that I can complete the 31 chapters of the text every five or six weeks or so. In a typical year, I can listen to the whole of the text about five or six times if I choose to. I highly recommend this approach to anyone who is interested in a deeper study of ACIM.

Ho'oponopono

Ho'oponopono is a Hawaiian healing process. At its simplest, the method consists of our repeating four short affirmations that characterize the essence of the approach (although there are many more involved ways into this too). We say the four phrases to the Divine within: *"I love you. I'm sorry. Please forgive me, and thank you."*

These phrases, repeated incessantly over time, clean out all kinds of negative personal and even collective toxicity accumulated in the psyche. In other words, the Ho'oponopono technique cleans out inter-generational or karmic toxicity that has accumulated in our psyches too. A simple everyday way of referring to Ho'oponopono is as CLEANING. In other words, we're using this technique to clean the psyche. We will be looking at cleaning more fully in the next chapter.

Brain Entrainment

Brain entrainment uses pulsing sound and or light energy to guide the mind into a desired brain wave state for optimal reprogramming. This entrainment can include binaural beats, which apply different rhythmic trance-inducing sounds in the left and right audio channels of one's headphones to create desired states of consciousness.

The theory is that the brain works at different frequencies in different states of consciousness. By listening to audio tracks at the frequency of the desired state of consciousness, we can help the brain or 'entrain' it, to reach the desired state for optimal transformation.

Virtual/Augmented Reality

Virtual reality and augmented reality are more immersive audio and video experiences. These generally involve wearing headgear to view fully immersive 360-degree video with high-quality audio. They may include subliminal messages and guided meditations and involve sophisticated simulations of the environments and states we desire to be in.

Nootropics

The concept of nootropics has been around since 1972, when Dr. Corneliu Giurgea coined the term. He described nootropics as

"...characterized by a direct functional activation of the higher integrative brain mechanisms that enhances cortical vigilance, a telencephalic functional selectivity, and a particular efficiency in restoring deficient higher nervous activity. In contradistinction to other psychotropic drugs, nootropics do not induce direct reticular, limbic, or other subcortical events." ("The Nootropic Concept and Its Prospective Implications," by Corneliu Giurgea in *Drug Development Research,* https://onlinelibrary. wiley.com/doi/abs/10.1002/ddr.430020505)

In layperson's terms, nootropics are natural or synthetic drugs or supplements which enhance mental performance without side effects or the possibility of addiction and withdrawal symptoms. They involve supposedly safe ways to stimulate the brain.

Scientific support for nootropics is still slim since many are derived from natural plant materials and are not patentable, thus of little interest to big pharma. The movie "Limitless" with Bradley Cooper is an interesting take on nootropics.

CHAPTER 5

CLEANING

*T-9.V.3. There is an advantage to bringing **nightmares** into awareness, but only to teach that they are not real, and that anything they contain is meaningless. 2 The unhealed healer cannot do this because he does not believe it. 3 All unhealed healers follow the ego's plan for forgiveness in one form or another. 4 If they are theologians, they are likely to condemn themselves, teach condemnation and advocate a fearful solution. 5 Projecting condemnation onto God, they make Him appear retaliative, and fear His retribution. 6 What they have done is merely to identify with the ego, and by perceiving what [it] does, condemn themselves because of this confusion. 7 It is understandable that there have been revolts against this concept, but to revolt against it is still to believe in it.*
—A Course in Miracles, T-9.V.3

Additional Familiar Frameworks

With the basics of The Nightmares to Miracles Program laid out so far, which involves the 3 Keys, the 4 Doors, The Integrated Model of the Psyche, and Mind Training, it is easy to plug in various additional frameworks as you already understand them. For instance, Stephen Covey's The *7 Habits of Highly Effective People* can be plugged in for

The Practical Key, as can Verne Harnish's *The Rockefeller Habits* and *Scaling Up*; Harville Hendrix's *Getting the Love You Want* can be plugged in for aspects of The Blueprint Key, while Ho'oponopono can be plugged in for other aspects of The Blueprint Key; and *A Course in Miracles,* either directly or in modified form, can be plugged into both The Blueprint Key and The Inner Genius Key.

In other words, there is no need to reinvent the wheel with this Nightmares to Miracles Program for other tools and resources you are already familiar with. The 3 Keys to Miracle Success can be likened to a kind of operating system, which, once installed, allows us to integrate all kinds of apps (i.e., other powerful frameworks) as needed.

In this book thus far, you have seen how significant *A Course in Miracles* has been in my awakening from Nightmares to Miracles and in my development of The Nightmares to Miracles Program being shared here. ACIM is a powerful resource for undoing the malicious ego and its toxic residue in the psyche. I remind you of my miraculous healing and recovery from a nearly catastrophic experience of congestive heart failure which I described in chapter 3, a miraculous recovery which I attribute in no small part to *A Course in Miracles*. Another powerful resource for undoing the ego's toxic residue in the psyche is Ho'oponopono, or as I like to call it, "Cleaning." We touched on this framework briefly in our review of Mind Training in the previous chapter. I draw heavily on Cleaning in my daily life and work, and we will look more closely at this now.

Ho'oponopono, or Cleaning

When we get stuck, there are usually subconscious psychological and spiritual issues involved in addition to the practical issues and blocks we must deal with.

To support more and faster breakthroughs in situations of blockage, I use a technique referred to as Ho'oponopono or cleaning that is of tremendous help.

Cleaning involves the incessant repetition of four basic affirmations (call them mantras if you like), as an ongoing mind training activity. The mantras are: *"I love you. I'm sorry. Please forgive me. Thank you."*

This works for specific situations but also for cleaning one's life more generally in a multidimensional and intergenerational way. I have used this technique with remarkable results in my own life and with clients.

This technique is known as Ho'oponopono (pronounced Ho-oh-po-noh-po-noh), and it originates from Hawaii. Ho'oponopono means "to make things right," which captures the purpose of our engaging in this mind training practice on a regular basis. The practice of Ho'oponopono or cleaning empowers to make things right in our lives.

I teach clients to use Ho'oponopono to clean childhood wounds, as described in *Getting the Love You Want* by Harville Hendrix and Helen Hunt. Although *Getting the Love You Want* is a guide for couples, I recommend it highly to everyone who will listen because of the excellent method in it for surfacing childhood wounds. These surfaced childhood wounds can then be cleaned using Ho'oponopono.

Childhood wounds refer to the deficits we experienced through those who parented us. No matter how well our parents did with us, there are going to have been deficits in how we experienced them loving us. They might have had a substance abuse problem. They might have been overworked. They might have been too lenient or too stern. They might have had hidden or glaring conflicts about love, money, sex, religion, politics, and so on. There are myriad things that could have impinged on us through our parents while we were growing up.

These wounds are the basis for repeating patterns throughout the rest of our lives, and especially in our romantic lives. We tend to attract and are attracted to people who recreate for us the emotional and psychological climate we experienced because of our childhood wounds. I recommend you read the chapters related to childhood wounds in *Getting the Love You Want*, then work with the exercises at the end of that book to surface your childhood wounds.

Once a client has become oriented to this approach of surfacing childhood wounds, I like to expand the concept more broadly into not only childhood wounds from parents but to all kinds of traumas, also starting in childhood. What I recommend, then, is keeping track of one's various wounds and traumas through an inventory which starts from zero to 10 years old, and where you record any childhood wounds in relation to those who parented you, together with any other painful experiences whatsoever. These could have been first or early sexual experiences that might have been overwhelming, scary, or inappropriate in some way. These could also have been experiences at school, with friends in the neighborhood, with bullies, nightmarish stories of crime and criminals in your area, illnesses, the death of loved ones, or one's own brushes with death, or any number of other traumatic experiences. Capture as many different traumatic experiences like these from that time in your life in some form of a written journal. Here the goal is not necessarily to write elaborately about these experiences (that can always be done later). Instead, the goal is to capture a list of as many painful experiences as possible from this time in your life.

Then, keep going with creating the inventory from ages 10 to 20, when we have all the growing pains related to the various coming of age rites of passages: going through adolescence, falling in love, ongoing sexual identity issues, various forms of experimentation, breaking away from the family unit to the peer group and so on. There can be all kinds of traumas from this period that we want to surface and create an inventory of.

Again, the inventory is more like a list of headline news items. We are not journaling extensively about these things right now. There is a time and a place for going into much more detail about these traumas. For now, we just want to record as many traumas that we might have experienced as possible. Now, keep the inventory process going from age 20 to 30, then from 30 to 40, up to as old as you might be now.

The point here is that in order to know in a fuller way what to clean on using the Hawaiian method of Ho'oponopono, we want to first resurface where the different pain points are throughout our life histories.

In the book *Zero Limits*, Joe Vitale and Dr. Hew Len work together to bring us a deeper understanding of the foundations of Ho'oponopono, how it functions, and what it is really doing for us.

The essence of their message is that the human psyche is like a computer on which is stored all kinds of data, including painful data and joyful data. In other words, there is all kinds of information stored on the computer hard drive that is the human psyche, with much of this information blocking the effective functioning of the computer.

This updated explanation of Ho'oponopono presented by Vitale and Len is about how to clean the human-computer of the information on it that blocks the computer's healthy functioning. At its simplest, the cleaning process, as has been mentioned earlier, is about the constant repetition of the following four mantras or affirmations: *"I love you, I'm sorry, please forgive me, and thank you."*

These are said over and over again to Higher Power (The Inner Genius) within us:

I love you, I'm sorry, please forgive me, and thank you.
I love you, I'm sorry, please forgive me, and thank you.
I love you, I'm sorry, please forgive me, and thank you.

This process cleans the psychological hard drive of accumulated toxic blocking information. You might ask, "Well, how exactly does cleaning do this? I don't get it."

I'll extend our computer metaphor to try and explain how this works. First of all, let's tweak the cleaning affirmations so that "I'm sorry" becomes "I'm stuck," and "Please forgive me" becomes "Please delete my negative programming which is keeping me stuck," and "Thank you" becomes "Thank you for getting me unstuck." Using these adjusted affirmations, the whole sequence of all four of them becomes *"I love you, I'm stuck, please delete my negative programming which is keeping me stuck, and thank you for getting me unstuck."*

Now imagine how in the 90s, when computers had glitches on them, or crashed, or were not working effectively, we used to call up tech support for help. Today you can usually do some quick searching on your smartphone and then use the instructions you find to diagnose your computer and get it functioning again in most cases. However, in the 90s, I routinely called computer tech support for help with most of my computer problems.

By using this earlier approach to computer tech support as a metaphor, the "I love you" affirmation is like the phone call that we make to computer tech support when we have a glitch on our computer. In the case of the toxic buildup, we're cleaning off our psychological hard drives; we're calling Divine tech support and not another human being for help. In other words, "I love you" is how we dial-in to Higher Power to initiate our request for assistance in fixing our glitchy psychological computer.

The "I'm sorry" affirmation is the next aspect of our call to Divine tech support. I've mentioned that this affirmation really means "I'm stuck" because of the toxic glitches on my psychological computer. For many of my clients, the "I'm sorry" affirmation sounds too much like we're beating ourselves up and wallowing in guilt with a "woe is me" quality to our attitude, which is not that productive. The essential point here is that we've tried to figure out how to get unstuck on our own rather than calling Divine tech support for help, and our own unproductive approach to the problem has resulted in wasted time and a lot of dead ends, and even nightmares for us. That is where the regret in the "I'm sorry" affirmation is coming from. Over time, I've found that a lot of my clients prefer the "I'm stuck" affirmation once they understand what the "I'm sorry" affirmation means. Nonetheless, you have a choice here: you can use the more traditional "I'm sorry" version of the affirmation or the version that I've reformulated into "I'm stuck."

So now that we've called Divine tech support ("I love you") and explained ("I'm stuck") to Divine tech support how blocked we are, and what all the issues are (as surfaced in the inventories of our traumas), including the regret we have in not calling for help faster and earlier, we're happy to be connected to Divine tech support in the knowledge that we're moving in the right direction towards getting the problem solved by competent assistance.

The next affirmation in the cleaning process is "Please forgive me," which can sound overly groveling or subservient to some people. The emphasis in this affirmation is on the phrase "forgive me," which here in this context technically means "release me," or "cut the chains that are binding me," or "unbind me from the burdens that are blocking me, that are causing me to be stuck." All of this essentially amounts to the following request to Divine tech support: "Please delete my negative programming, which is keeping me stuck." However, when we repeat the affirmations rapidly and incessantly, we don't necessarily need to repeat the "which is keeping me stuck" portion of the affirmation, which can be assumed.

It is crucial for this cleaning process that we make our request for cleaning assistance explicitly to Divine tech support because divine power will not clean out the accumulated toxicity on our psychological hard drives if we do not explicitly request this assistance.

This step in the cleaning process is like the procedure that was followed with actual human-computer tech support. At some point in our call to human tech support, the technician would check in with us in a manner similar to the following: "Can I get on your computer remotely? Do I have your permission to get on your computer? When I'm on your computer, it'll just be for this session, and what I do on your computer will be limited to the specific problem you told me about. In other words, I'm not going to maintain indefinite, ongoing access to your computer. I'm not going to roam around doing what I want on your computer. I'm simply here at your invitation to fix the things that you've told me you are having trouble with, and nothing else."

The procedure is essentially the same with Divine tech support. We have free agency, and free will, and autonomy. The bottom line is that the Divine is too gracious and too respectful of things that we have accumulated on our hard drive simply to barge in and start cleaning house. The Divine only cleans through the specific permissions that we grant for doing so.

The final part of the Divine cleaning process, as with human tech support, if it goes well, is usually an enormous sense of gratitude and relief that there is competent help to fix our problems. Also, as we engage Divine tech support in the cleaning process, often we can feel that the cleaning is happening; we begin to feel lighter and not as blocked as before we started the cleaning. The natural response to such powerful assistance is gratitude: "Thank you." As I mentioned earlier, I've reformulated this expression of gratitude into the following: "Thank you for getting me unstuck."

After I introduce clients to cleaning and explain the above tech support metaphor, I coach them to do five rounds of each of the affirmations out loud with me. You can do this by yourself now too.

Just repeat each one of these affirmations five times. Try the older, more traditional approach, and then the newer version I formulated so you see how each version feels to you and which you prefer as the main approach in your emerging and growing practice of cleaning.

So, first, repeat the affirmations in the older, more traditional approach as follows:

I love you.
I love you.
I love you.
I love you.
I love you.

I'm sorry.
I'm sorry.
I'm sorry.
I'm sorry.
I'm sorry.

Please forgive me.

Please forgive me.
Please forgive me.
Please forgive me.
Please forgive me.

Thank you.
Thank you.
Thank you.
Thank you.
Thank you.

Now repeat the affirmations in my reformulated version:

I love you.
I love you.
I love you.
I love you.
I love you.

I'm stuck.
I'm stuck.
I'm stuck.
I'm stuck.
I'm stuck.

Please delete my negative programming.
Please delete my negative programming.
Please delete my negative programming.
Please delete my negative programming.
Please delete my negative programming.

Thank you for getting me unstuck.
Thank you for getting me unstuck.
Thank you for getting me unstuck.
Thank you for getting me unstuck.

Thank you for getting me unstuck.

You now have these two different approaches to cleaning. I am comfortable with both of them and regularly use both approaches to clean out the toxicity on my psychological hard drive regularly. The newer way that I've formulated includes the explanations that I've given in trying to help get people on board with this. Feel free to use either approach as you see fit.

Morrnah's Prayer

Ho'oponopono also includes a longer prayer called Morrnah's Prayer. This longer prayer is what has been boiled down over time in Hawaiian practice to the four affirmations or mantras. I believe it's useful at this point to explore Morrnah's Prayer just a bit to see more of what's entailed in the cleaning process. Morrnah's Prayer is as follows:

> *Divine creator, father, and mother, son as one,*
> *if I, my family, relatives, and ancestors*
> *have offended you, your family, relatives, and ancestors*
> *in thoughts, words, deeds, and actions,*
> *from the beginning of our creation to the present,*
> *we ask your forgiveness. Let this cleanse purify, release, and*
> *   cut off*
> *all the negative memories, blocks, energies, and vibrations,*
> *and transmute these unwanted energies into pure light, and*
> *   it is done.*

The first line, "Divine creator," is the dialing into divine tech support, as I discussed earlier in relation to the affirmation, "I love you.".

Then the prayer splits the communication to the Divine creator into father and mother, and son while recognizing that they are all functioning as one. Father is often considered the part of the psyche known as the superconscious mind (i.e., what we've been referring to as The Inner Genius), the mother is frequently thought of as the part of the psyche that is the conscious mind, and son or child is frequently thought of as the part of the psyche that is the subconscious mind. Putting all of this together, thus far, we have that the prayer asks the Divine, at the three levels of mind (the superconscious level, the conscious level, and the subconscious level), to get involved and to start the cleaning and healing process within the psyche.

The prayer then pivots from addressing the Divine creator to both the creator and anyone else that we may have problems with of any kind. The phrase, "If I, my family, relatives, and ancestors," is a comprehensive catch-all phrase intended to capture as many aspects of the accumulated toxic grievances in our family line as possible. This phrase means we recognize our complicity in the faults of others in our various lineages who have done wrong to others, as well as that we have a responsibility to fix (through Divine cleaning) problems generated within our various ancestral lineages and family linkages.

Next, the prayer says the following: "have offended you, your family, or your relatives and ancestors." Here the prayer provides an equally thorough roundup of all those we or our "kin" might have harmed or offended in some way. This could refer to the Divine whom we may have attacked in various ways, or it could refer to someone we consider an individual enemy, a family enemy, a tribal enemy, or a national enemy, for example.

The prayer continues with this phrase: "in thoughts, words, deeds, and actions." Again, quite a comprehensive catch-all phrase covering all the bases regarding any harm we may have caused.

The next part of the prayer is as follows: "From the beginning of our creation to the present." Again, this is a pretty comprehensive approach to any harm we may have caused. It's like scooping up any mistake, any problem, any offense, anything that we've done wrong to anybody from the beginning of when we were actually created. Not just born, but from the beginning of creation—you can even go as far back as to the Big Bang if you want. This part of the prayer is about going as deeply inter-generationally as you can possibly imagine.

The next part of the prayer is as follows: "we ask your forgiveness." As mentioned earlier, forgiveness here means we're asking to be set free from the toxic chains that bind us. This cleaning process is like having a big and powerful delete button on the computer. It just removes everything negative, toxic, and undesirable in our psychological "files." As mentioned earlier, you could also think of cleaning as enabling us to go back to restore points on our psychological computers or even enabling us to go back to a factory reset. These are all different concepts that we have in contemporary computer culture captured by the cleaning processes and prayers of Ho'oponopono.

Next, the prayer says the following: "Let this cleanse, purify, release, cut all the negative vibrations." It is our request for forgiveness or release, and the Divine's ability to release us that this phrase is amplifying about our understanding of this process of release.

Next, we have another set of very comprehensive phrases: "...the negative memories, blocks, energies, and vibrations...."

Here we are asking the Divine to cut all the chains that bind us, all the negatives, all the problems and nightmares besetting us. This forgiveness is about releasing us from all that ails us. The Divine has the power to do this for us, but only if we ask to be released. That is what that word, "forgiveness," here means – i.e., release from any and all negative elements related to the specific issue(s) we are seeking help about.

Then, next, unless we're in any doubt about what we are requesting and what we are receiving, the prayer says, "Please transmute all of these unwanted energies into pure light, and it is done."

This is a very comprehensive, thorough cleaning prayer. I have a recording of the prayer, which chants it multiple times on an eight-minute audio that you can download for $0.99 from iTunes (see the appendix for a link where you can obtain this audio). I have put this audio program in my car, in my bathroom, and on my phones. Whenever I have a significant amount of time not dedicated to some other type of mind training or visualizing, or something else, I go for 30 minutes, an hour, sometimes two or three hours, just chanting this cleaning prayer. I clean out pockets of difficulty that I remember, or I just clean in a general way for even deeper healing of things that I might not even fully recall.

In addition to Morrnah's Prayer, the iTunes audio listed in the appendix has the four cleaning affirmations on it too, and these are repeated a number of times: *"I love you. I'm sorry. Please forgive me. And thank you."* What cleaning practice do you think you might like to commit to?

CHAPTER 6

THE GOALS GRID

T-9.V.4.Some newer forms of the ego's plan are as unhelpful as the older ones, because form does not matter and the content has not changed. 2 In one of the newer forms, for example, a psychotherapist may interpret the ego's symbols in a nightmare, and then use them to prove that the nightmare is real. 3 Having made it real, he then attempts to dispel its effects by depreciating the importance of the dreamer. 4 This would be a healing approach if the dreamer were also identified as unreal. 5 Yet if the dreamer is equated with the mind, the mind's corrective power through the Holy Spirit is denied. 6 This is a contradiction even in the ego's terms, and one which it usually notes even in its confusion.
—**A Course in Miracles, T-9.V.4**

The Goals Grid is the first stage of an efficient and easy-to-use system that combines The 3 Keys with The 4 Doors for maximum effectiveness towards miracle success.

Print out a copy of The Goals Grid and fill it in. You can find The Goals Grid and all the other images and worksheets at this link:

https://bit.ly/3tmMMjx
password: n2m

You must copy and paste the link for it to work; just clicking on it doesn't work. Also please reformat worksheets such as the Goals Grid to give you more room to write your entries in.

If you'd like a digital version to fill in, please request one from me at dasomaning@synchromind.com.

HEALTH	WEALTH, BUSINESS, PROFESSIONAL, CAREER	LOVE	ENLIGHTENMENT
Practical Goals	Practical Goals	Practical Goals	Practical Goals
"I set and achieve clear, ambitious and measurable goals"			
1	1	1	1
2	2	2	2
BLUEPRINTS TO ELIMINATE	BLUEPRINTS TO ELIMINATE	BLUEPRINTS TO ELIMINATE	BLUEPRINTS TO ELIMINATE
"I AM aware of and undo my negative blueprints"			
1	1	1	1
2	2	2	2
Cleaning:1.I love you 2.I'm stuck 3.Please delete my negative programming 4.Thank you for getting me unstuck			
INNER GENIUS	INNER GENIUS	INNER GENIUS	INNER GENIUS
"I AM aware of and use the guidance, strength, and plan of the Inner Genius in what I think, Say, and do"			
1	1	1	1
2	2	2	2
HEALTH - L 136	WEALTH - L 97	LOVE - L 121	ENLIGHTENMENT - L41 & L44
Sickness is a defense against the TRUTH	Spirit AM I; a holy child of God; free of all limits;safe and healed and whole; free to forgive and free to save the world (half billion return for every 5 minutes spent)	Forgiveness is the key to happiness	L41 God goes with me wherever I go L44 God is the light in which I see

GOALS GRID

GOAL-SETTING FOR 20___

Here's a quick overview of how to use this grid effectively. Using the lists of goals you created in previous chapters , choose your top two health goals and write them in The Health column under The Practical Goals header.

Then move down to The Blueprint box and enter two negative patterns that you would most like to change related to your health. When you have written them down, say the four phrases from Ho'oponopono to yourself: *"I love you, I'm stuck, please delete my negative programming, and thank you for getting me unstuck."* These phrases assist us in removing the negative psychological programming at the root of our negative blueprint patterns.

Next, move down to The Inner Genius box, and internalize the affirmation provided from Lesson 136 of *A Course in Miracles* (ACIM): *"Sickness is a defense against the Truth."* Because I am an avid student and teacher of ACIM, I use tools from ACIM, but please feel free to plug in similar affirmations from the religious or spiritual path you feel most comfortable with.

Repeat the process with your wealth goals, then with your love goals, then with your enlightenment goals. See how simple this is as an approach to integrating The 3 Keys with The 4 Doors? Now we'll go over everything in The Goals Grid in more detail.

The Health Column

Starting with health, you are going to have a couple of practical goals. Then you are going to have a couple of blueprint dynamics to eliminate, and then you are going to use the wisdom of your Inner Genius to heal. So, you have The 3 Keys focusing specifically on health.

Just to use a quick example, let's say your health goal is as follows: "I want to lose 30 pounds in the next six months." That is a very concrete goal. It is clear, ambitious, and measurable. So that goes in line #1 in The Practical Key of the Health Box. For line #2, imagine a goal to reduce meal portions.

In The Blueprint Key, think of the goal in line #1 and what the parallel blueprint to be eliminated is. A blueprint concern might be, "The people in my family are all heavy," or "I've been heavy all my life." You then enter this blueprint issue in line #1 of the box for The Blueprint Key under the Health column to keep track of the fact that it's a blueprint issue about the goal of losing 30 pounds. For the goal on line #2, the blueprint issue might be, "I love eating, and I love the different tastes of food, and I don't want to give up that experience." That could be a blueprint program blocking you with regard to reducing portion sizes.

You could have many more than two goals and their two corresponding blueprint issues here, but for the purpose of illustrating how to fill the grid out, I want to keep things as simple as possible.

You will be looking at this grid every day and applying this affirmation for The Practical Key: *"I set and achieved clear, ambitious and measurable goals."* Then with your blueprint entries, you will remind yourself, "I'm aware of and undo my negative blueprints."

As you do this consistently every day, you will also add a bit of cleaning to your regimen, saying, *"I love you, I'm stuck, please delete my negative programming, thank you for getting me unstuck."* Or if you prefer the traditional version of cleaning that we looked at earlier, you can say *"I love you, I'm sorry, please forgive me, thank you."*

Regarding The Inner Genius Key and that portion of the grid, the affirmation is, *"I am aware of and use the guidance, strength, and plan of The Inner Genius in what I think, say and do."* Not only are you setting the goals and being determined to achieve them, but you are also turbocharging these goals even more by dropping unconscious sabotaging patterns that you might have, and then also plugging into Divine Power within to provide you with additional strength and guidance.

When you name obstacles, like, "My family is heavy," or, "I like eating too much, and I don't want to give it up," those blueprints are just the tip of the iceberg. There are so many additional subconscious impediments, so many layers that have to be cleaned on. The good news is that a little bit of cleaning goes a long way. But we do have to do it incessantly for, say, weeks or even months at a time. With The Inner Genius, not only are we cleaning and drawing on Divine Power to help us, but now we are also moving into some deeper miracle principles and practices.

At the bottom of the Health column of The Goals Grid, you'll notice an entry—Lesson 136—which is from *A Course in Miracles*. The headline for that lesson is, "Sickness is a defense against the truth."

What this means is that any kind of malaise (whether it's having too much weight, overeating, having portions that are too big, not exercising enough, or even including heart problems, cancer, and other serious conditions) is caused by a deep inner subconscious decision to be sick.

This lesson, Lesson 136, is extraordinarily helpful in cutting to the chase and undoing an enormous amount of negativity through the help of a higher power within, God, Jesus, Buddha—however, you want to characterize the Divine Source.

A disclaimer here: I am not giving medical advice. I am not saying you should not see your doctor or take your doctor's advice. You should. I was under the care of a physician when I was using all of this to help me out of the catastrophic, deadly situation with congestive heart failure in 2014.

So, when it says, "Sickness is a defense against the truth," the truth is that we are perfect, and the malicious ego we have talked about is the culprit trying to get us to believe we are the limitations we see in our physical natures, in our bodies.

The ego gets us to forget we are perfect creatures, at the level of spirit, and it uses the ailments and fragility of the body as a defense to block us from understanding and accepting and living in the truth of our limitlessness, our freedom from all limits, in the spirit.

Sickness thus becomes an idol, or a shrine of the ego, a state of mind where we set sickness in motion and engage in various unconscious maneuvers to preserve the state of sickness. I am not saying we should blame people who are sick. We do not kick people when they are down. I am not saying negative things like that. ACIM teaches that we choose to be sick, to block our own access to the truth about our limitlessness and spirit. So the emphasis in ACIM is not in blaming ourselves or others for our problems, but rather affirming that we can wake up from the nightmare we are in by unmasking and neutralizing the underlying dynamics of the malicious ego causing the problems.

That is what it means to say that sickness is a defense against the truth. Once we penetrate this defense, understand it, and disarm it, healing results come almost automatically, and this is what happened with my heart problem.

I was, in some ways, holding onto a fantasy of all the benefits I would get subconsciously by having this dire catastrophic illness. You can get a lot of attention when you're sick, at least in the beginning, until people begin to get tired of you. You get a timeout; you get to be a martyr. Once we recognize these distorted and hidden motivations and are willing to relinquish them, we experience the easing of our symptoms and can enjoy restored health.

The Wealth Column

Now we move to the Wealth, Business/Professional/Career column, and here, you might set the goal of doubling or tripling your annual income or paying off all your debts or having a nice nest egg for retirement, or something else. Maybe you want to purchase a house, or a new car, or achieve any number of other financial goals.

The point is to aim to get into robust financial health by setting clear goals in all the different areas of financial well-being, from income to bills, to debt, to savings, to investments, and others. The crucial thing to remember when setting your goals is to have concrete numbers in mind.

So let's say your income goal is to earn $100,000 a year. There is no judgment about your target. The important thing is to set the target for yourself. I encourage my clients to do this, and I do it myself —the more ambitious, the better, for a lot of reasons.

Write down $100,000 as your #1 goal in the practical box of the Wealth column. Then your #2 goal might be a debt reduction goal, improving your credit, launching your business, taking your business from five figures to six figures, to seven to eight figures, then to nine figures, and so on.

The blueprints to eliminate for your income in goal #1, in the example here, could be any of the following: "I've been stuck in scarcity for so long, I don't think I'll ever get out of it. It seems like I'm cursed, or I'm jinxed, or I'm doomed." These are some patterns I encounter often in clients.

If goal #2 in wealth has to do with building your business, your blueprint issue might be any of the following: "You need money to make money, and I don't have money, and so I'll never get anywhere. I'll never be successful in my business because I don't have access to any capital."

As we did with the health category, we're surfacing these various financial blueprint issues so that we can undo them using the cleaning phrases: *"I love you, I'm stuck, please delete my negative programming, thank you for getting me unstuck."*

After the cleaning process in The Blueprint box of The Health column, we proceed to The Inner Genius box, using the main affirmation there as follows: *"I am aware of and use the guidance, strength, and plan of The Inner Genius in what I think, say and do [about my wealth goals....and the related blueprint issues]."*

In The Wealth column, I apply Lesson 97 from *A Course in Miracles.* Part of this lesson goes as follows: "Spirit am I, a Holy Child of God, free of all limits, safe and healed and whole, free to forgive, and free to save the world."

I have a mastermind group devoted to *A Course in Miracles*, and we studied Lesson 97 for the whole of 2017. It was the single lesson we kept coming back to, month after month, throughout the year. As we studied this lesson from month to month in 2017, I began to get in touch with what I now call the "Miracle Math," embedded in the lesson. In summary, this lesson promises that for every five minutes you spend meditating on and remembering your true identity as a Holy Child of God, who is free of all limits; who is safe, healed, and whole; and extending this limitlessness mentally to the rest of the world, you're reducing the amount of time humanity will continue to suffer by thousands and even tens of thousands of years. If you do the math related to this promise, it means for every 5 minutes you spend meditating on your Divine limitlessness, you receive a return on that minimal effort that amounts to almost a billion minutes (i.e., tens of thousands of years of reduced suffering for humanity). In other words, this lesson promises that for every 5 minutes spent in meditation on our Divine limitlessness, that time will be leveraged, not just exponentially but astronomically. That's such an amazing return on investment (ROI). The return on investment involved here makes it a no-brainer to spend this type of meditation time throughout the day. It seems to make sense to extend our thinking about this amazing type of ROI and apply this type of ROI to other types of investments, including our financial ones too.

This is why in the Wealth column in the ACIM section, I've noted in parentheses there that conservatively, you receive a "half-billion return for every 5 minutes spent." While this is admittedly about spiritual uplift and liberation for ourselves as individuals and humanity as a whole, as we practice these 5-minute meditations, I'm convinced that the principle applies to all areas of well-being, including financial success. This lesson, Lesson 97, is worth repeatedly studying for the amazing things it teaches and promises about astronomical ROIs in all areas of well-being.

The Love Column

Shifting to Love, you have space on the grid to write down some of your practical goals. For some people, it is to find their soulmate, get married, and start a family. For others, it is to leave an unsatisfactory or dysfunctional, or abusive relationship. For others it is to remain happily single.

These would be your #1 and #2 goals. Again, there are endless practical goals in the realm of love, not limited to romantic love or family love. There is neighborhood love, love of the city you live in, your country, the world. There is love for all living things, including plants and animals, and the very Earth itself.

So there are many diverse levels of love where we can set our goals. Some of these goals can also translate into philanthropy in which we raise and employ money for significant and meaningful charitable endeavors.

Here as well, we consider the blueprints that we plan to eliminate. So, number one could be, "I've been hurt too many times, I'll never find love," or, "All men are X, Y, and Z, so it's never going to work," or, "All women are X, Y, and Z," or, "I'm way too conflicted about my orientation, or my gender, or my status. I don't know what I'm doing."

There are a number of ways to identify your negative blueprints in this area. You may also add things like, "I didn't have good role models growing up, in how my mother or my father were with each other," for example. Again, the goal is to become aware of and undo negative blueprints; remembering that whatever you connect with regarding such negative patterns is most likely just the tip of the iceberg.

Here again, we have some cleaning to do using the following phrases: *"I love you, I'm stuck, please delete my negative programming, and thank you for getting me unstuck."* At The Inner Genius level of love, we are again using the affirmation, "I am aware of and use the guidance, strength, and plan of The Inner Genius, in what I think, say and do."

Also, for each of these Inner Genius levels in Health, Wealth, Love, and Enlightenment, in addition to the lesson that I'm providing from *A Course in Miracles*, there is room for a #1 and #2 spiritual practice of your own that you may want to make note of.

This is where you will write in the practices you are willing to engage in. There might be a hypnosis program you are interested in using, a specific meditation technique, or a prayer, so that is what each number in this section is for. It stands for your commitment to some sort of mind training activity, in addition to everything presented here, that will help you to tune in to your Inner Genius in relation to the column for The Door to Miracle Success you are currently working on filling details in for.

These practices can repeat through Health and Wealth and Love and Enlightenment. While these could be the same practices throughout or different ones, it is crucial to have them noted here in The Goals Grid so that when you review this every day, before your day really gets going, this grid and the practices you have noted down become a regular part of your daily mind training.

For The Love column, in The Inner Genius category, Lesson 121, from *A Course in Miracles,* says, "Forgiveness is the key to happiness," and there is an exercise in this lesson, which I refer to as "the triangle of light" exercise.

In the first part of the exercise, you picture somebody you consider to be an enemy or a problem in your life. Then you visualize a light somewhere in this person. We are visualizing their body, and then we see a light gradually expanding to cover their whole body.

The second part of the exercise is to transfer this light from this person we dislike to somebody we consider a friend, somebody that we feel positively towards or that we have good feelings towards.

I usually use Jesus and see that light transfer to Jesus from whomever I've chosen as my enemy for that particular practice session. The third part of the exercise is to transfer the light from your friend to yourself, or in my case in the example above, from Jesus to myself.

Now you've established a triangle of light in your psyche. First, you see a light in your so-called enemy, and this light grows, and then the light shifts to a person you consider a friend, and then, that light shifts back to you. You can keep circulating the light in this triangle of light. You can also include more people in that triangle to create a circle of light. If you wanted to, you could include your pets, nature, or the like.

The Enlightenment Column

Finally, in The Goals Grid, we have The Enlightenment column. A practical and recommended goal here is to work through all 365 lessons of *A Course in Miracles*, that is, to practice one lesson a day but not to do more than one lesson a day. These are the basic instructions in ACIM, although you can stick with one lesson for longer than a day.

If you do a lesson for two or three days, it might take you several years to finish the whole course, although it's normally intended that it be finished in a year. But I know many people, including myself, who have had to linger with a lesson for more than a day because there is so much to absorb, take in, and practice.

Let us say your first goal is to finish all 365 lessons. Then, you might find you have some sort of a negative habit that is slowing you down in life. It could be drinking or smoking, or any other habit you feel is impeding your spiritual progress.

Even though it seems like a health issue, it is also something that you are concerned about, as an obstacle to your enlightenment. You might put it down in The Enlightenment column as a goal you want to work on.

Blueprints to eliminate in this Enlightenment column might include: "doing 365 lessons of ACIM just seems so dense. I don't understand it, it seems too difficult, it seems beyond me." Or, about bad habits, "That's how I medicate myself; it soothes me when I'm stressed out. I don't want to give it up."

There is no judgment about any of these blueprint patterns. The goal is to connect with what they are. Some people say, "I just feel too lazy; I just don't want to put that much effort into it." Or some people say, "I start, then I stop. I start, then I stop."

Whatever the blueprint issues are, write them down without judgment, and then clean on them again, as we have described how to do before: *"I love you, I'm stuck, please delete my negative programming. Thank you for getting me unstuck."*

In addition to what we have covered here thus far, there might be one or two further mind training techniques you find to incorporate into your daily regimen in some way. These additional techniques can be fairly quick ones to use. So for example, I have a 20-minute guided meditation that I am able to use across the board for all of these components of The Goals Grid.

You will learn to mix and match different techniques and tools so that they fit the time available to you at the start of your day as you go through your Goals Grid regimen. Some people can only start with 10 minutes, some have 30 minutes, and some have an hour or even two hours available for daily mind training. You can tailor the daily regime involved in all this to suit your available time and then expand and evolve how you practice, step by step, to include more elements that are helpful to you.

In The Enlightenment column, Lesson 41 of ACIM says, "God goes with me wherever I go," and Lesson 44 says, "God is the light in which I see"—both excellent expressions for an Enlightenment goal. So, here we are picturing God as The Source of the true light that enables us to see everything in truth and clarity everywhere we go and in everything we do.

Complete your entries into your Goals Grid and look at it at the beginning of your day. It won't take you more than five minutes to survey everything. You see all your practical goals in Health, Wealth, Love, and Enlightenment. You see all your blueprint impediments, again, in Health, Wealth, Love, and Enlightenment. Then, you see all the ways in which The Inner Genius is going to take everything and turbocharge it for you astronomically so that you will go from achieving, slow, or even unsatisfactory results, and in many cases, nightmarish kinds of experiences, to miracle breakthroughs.

The important point here is to look at your Goals Grid every day, even if just for five minutes. You want to review everything quickly, do the cleaning, do the exercises that the ACIM lessons refer to, do your own additional mind training through a hypnosis program or a subliminal program, in doing all this, put together your own recipe for practicing your daily regimen. By doing your mind training every day, you will see your practice grow and evolve in leaps and bounds, and thereby, you will experience many Nightmares to Miracles breakthroughs in the areas of your life you need and want them.

CHAPTER 7

THE 1-PAGE MIND TRAINER

*T.9.V.7.4 The only meaningful contribution the healer can make is to present an example of one whose direction has been changed [for] [him], and who no longer believes in **nightmares** of any kind.*
—A Course in Miracles, T-9.V.7.4

The 1-Page Mind Trainer is a 3 Keys-based tool that brings everything we are working on right in front of us in summary form every day. We look at The 1-Page Mind Trainer every day to strengthen our move towards our cleaning and fixing those problems, patterns, glitches, and mistakes that hold us back.

The 1-Page Mind Trainer is 3 Keys-based. It consists of three columns left to right—The Practical Key, The Blueprint Key, and The Inner Genius Key

The Practical Key column has three sections: a section for our goals, a section for our recent achievements, and a section called "The Parking Lot," where we put things that are of more distant, albeit significant, interest to us.

The Blueprint Key column has two sections. The first is about the current stressors in our lives, as well as the current problems we are trying to solve. The second section is about the various traumas we have suffered along the way in life.

The Inner Genius Key column also has two sections. The first section is about our areas of genius, talent, and passion, together with a feature I refer to as "exponentials," which we will go into more fully in a bit. The second section I refer to as our miracle resume and is about all the miracles we have experienced throughout our lives to date.

In addition to these main components, The 1-Page Mind Trainer has a few additional affirmations and sentence completions intended to keep us focused on being, and staying, miracle-minded at all times and in all things.

I call this document a "mind trainer" in line with ACIM's use of the idea of mind training, which is about constantly bringing the mind back to the Divine, to Higher Power, to Spirit even as the mind seeks to wander back into the ego at every turn. The 1-Page Mind Trainer is a comprehensive document to aid our all-out, incessant focus of the mind on our best and highest intended outcomes in all areas of our lives. It's intended to be like a pilot's brief flight plan. You look at your flight plan at the beginning of the day before you really get moving; a flight plan with everything that's important to you about where you're headed in life, and you say, "Okay, this is what my day is going to be organized by. All the things represented here in this document are elements of what will guide and direct my flight through the day, as I make this day and every day really count towards my ultimate destination in life."

You might be asking, "Well how is The 1-Page Mind Trainer any different from the Goals Grid we developed and explored in chapter 6?" There are a couple of answers to this question. First, the goals grid focuses mainly on how we apply The 3 Keys to The 4 Doors in an organized and fairly comprehensive manner. Second, the Goals Grid is a building block we use in The 1-Page Mind Trainer; meaning also that The 1-Page Mind Trainer is a more comprehensive snapshot of psyches. And third, The 1-Page Mind Trainer is intended to be the basis of our digital vision board or treasure map; everything before this has been important prep work to arrive at this final document.

Let us now turn more fully to each of the components on The 1-Page Mind Trainer.

THE PRACTICAL KEY	THE BLUEPRINT KEY	THE INNER GENIUS KEY
"I set and achieve clear, ambitious, and measurable goals"	"I am aware of and undo my negative blueprints" [Cleaning: "I love you, I'm stuck, Please delete my negative programming, Thank You"]	"I am aware of and use the guidance, strength, and plan of the Inner Genius in what I think, say, and do"
MAIN GOAL AREAS FOR 2019 1. Health	STRESS BOX & CURRENT PROBLEMS TO BE SOLVED •	GENIUS AREAS: AREAS OF SPECIAL TALENT AND/OR PASSION & EXPONENTIALS
2. Wealth	•	•
3. Love	MAIN TRAUMAS STARTING IN CHILDHOOD	• MIRACLE RESUME: AMAZING EXPERIENCES FROM CHILDHOOD ON
4. Enlightenment	•	•
RECENT ACHIEVEMENTS	•	•
•	THE 4 DOORS TO MIRACLE SUCCESS	
•	**Health** | *"I now manifest and enjoy optimal health in all areas of my life"*	
•	**Wealth** | *"I am now a miracle-minded enterprise leader"* (e.g., CEO, Other Executive, Entrepreneur, Millionaire, Mover and Shaker, etc.)	
PARKING LOT	**Love** | *"I now manifest and enjoy my optimal relationship(s) with_____guilt-free"*	
•	**Enlightenment** | *"I AM Enlightened, and I now manifest and enjoy optimal peace"*	
•	MIRACLES | *"Miracles are solutions to problems that seem impossible to solve"*	
•	**For Miracles, Ask the Inner Genius** | *"What's the fastest, easiest, and smartest way for me to_____?"*	
	"I am entitled to miracles" | *"I practice meditating, with my Inner Genius, 5 minutes of every hour, throughout the day"*	

1-PAGE MIND TRAINER

I have also created a PowerPoint version of The 1-Page Mind Trainer, which includes subliminal and hypnotic imagery. This is available from dasomaning@synchromind.com.

Goals

The best place to start when it comes to filling in and using The 1-Page Mind Trainer is with the goals box. Keeping in mind the affirmation for The Practical Key, which is, "I set and achieve clear, ambitious, and measurable goals," we clarify and write down in goals box our health goals, our wealth goals, our love goals, and our enlightenment goals. In other words, we set clear, ambitious, and measurable goals for The 4 Doors to Miracle Success.

If you've already completed your Goals Grid from chapter 6, then you're simply transferring what you have there into The 1-Page Mind Trainer. If you're coming directly to The 1-Page Mind Trainer without having completed your Goals Grid, then the following applies to you. Starting with health, perhaps we would like to lose a few pounds, eat healthier foods, and exercise more. Exactly what measures do we intend to use for each of these sub-goals in our program to get healthier? When do we intend to have achieved these goals? And what plan or process are we willing to invest in to reach our goals?

Perhaps we have a health goal of doing something super ambitious like preparing for triathlons, or going to the Olympics, or doing some other type of intensive training to step up our health and fitness. Perhaps, we are deep in a health nightmare of some kind, such as addiction, obesity, or some so-called terminal condition in which the experts have given us 3 months, 6 months, a year, or 3 years to live. Our goal in any of these nightmare scenarios is to go from the nightmare to miracles, i.e., to reverse the dire circumstances of the path we are currently on.

In all of these situations, we start with the goal we desire to achieve, no matter how ridiculous or outlandish it may seem to us or to others. We simply put down in the goals box what it is we desire to achieve in a short, easy-to-remember way, together with some information about the metrics related to the goal, which is usually about "how much, by when, doing what?

Having and achieving our health goals as outlined above will itself help us to be much better leaders. Nonetheless, there are also specific leadership goals we want to capture as we look at the next door to miracle success, i.e., The Wealth Door. It includes our work, professions, and careers, as well as entrepreneurship and other forms of work-based leadership.

One classic example of setting goals in this area I use when I think of my own goals and when I am supporting executives and other leaders I work with to think in very big ways about their leadership goals is to take a look at President John F. Kennedy's moonshot goals. Most people know aspects of this story. In the late 1950s, the Soviet Union was ahead of the United States in the space race. This had dire implications for the United States regarding the nuclear arms race, as all the best practices achieved in space travel would redound to the benefit of supremacy in the nuclear arms race for the country winning the space race.

In the initial stages of the space race, while the Soviets were effectively putting satellites into the Earth's orbit on a regular basis, the United States was stuck in a pattern of abject failure when it came even just to launching various rockets. You can find videos showing one failure after another of the United States' attempts to launch its rockets in the early stages of its space program. These videos of early failure are somewhat amusing despite the dire consequences at stake.

Amidst this dire situation came President Kennedy, who, as a leader, declared to the world that the United States was going do whatever it would take to send people to the Moon and return them to Earth safely within the decade. Here we have what is now a legendary example of having a moonshot, i.e., a hugely ambitious goal that would take care of a lot of problems while seeming impossible to achieve.

The term moonshot has now entered popular parlance around Silicon Valley startups and Unicorns. They all have distinctive moonshots for what they intend to do in business terms while at the same time working to solve some major human problems related to as education, poverty, pollution, climate change, energy, terrorism, and so on.

What are your moonshots as a leader? As I like to say, aim for the stars and reach the moon. In other words, learn to have astronomically huge goals. While such goals may not be achievable right now (i.e., like going to other stars), the habitual attempt to figure out solutions to such seemingly impossible assignments will help us to achieve extraordinary results in the shorter term, i.e., such as getting us to the Moon.

When it comes to making money at a basic level or at extremely high levels of wealth-creation, I often like to hear from clients what their responses are to the "how much, by when, doing what" questions. I recommend putting some of your answers to these questions down in the goal box of The 1-Page Mind Trainer.

In work and career, a related question for many, is "How do I get on the path of my true purpose and calling in life?" I ask for a couple of points to be documented on the 1-Page Mind Trainer about what you are good at and what you've had success at in the past. Some of this becomes clearer also when you've made your entries in the two boxes for The Inner Genius Key section of The 1-Page Mind Trainer.

At this point, you may be asking, "How do I put all this information on The 1-Page Mind Trainer without making everything so small it hurts my eyes? This question is a problem that has been deliberately built into the process of developing and using The 1-Page Mind Trainer on an on-going basis.

On a basic level, you can develop several 1-Page Mind Trainers for specific topics, so you might have one dedicated to health, another one dedicated to career and wealth, another dedicated to love, and yet another dedicated to enlightenment. While you can do this, if everything seems too cramped, I suggest you keep in mind that The 1-Page Mind Trainer is a quick summary of everything about you all in one place.

Another way I respond to the question about what to do about everything being so cramped on The 1-Page Mind Trainer is by way of a metaphor. Imagine that your 1-Page Mind Trainer is a prototype of a smartphone. As with a smartphone, you are constrained to a certain size. Once it gets bigger than that, it is no longer a smartphone with its advantages of mobility, ubiquity, and convenience. If you make it bigger, it becomes a tablet, or when made bigger still, a PC. Part of our challenge with The 1-Page Mind Trainer is to keep it contained and make it a game in which every day we discover better ways to make this single page capture and do everything we want it to capture and do for us with regard to its being a map of our best lives possible.

In actual smartphone technology, one way the smartphone's space is extended without limit is by the introduction of apps. What is the equivalent of this with The 1 Page Mind Trainer? Giving this problem to your mind to solve daily as you use your 1-Page Mind Trainer will support you to continue to think and grow in unlimited ways.

When it comes to the third Door of Success, *Love*, what are your goals? Do you want to be single? Do you want to be married? Do you want to have children? In the case of marriage and children, when do you want to achieve these goals? What type of partner are you most interested in? By when do you want to be partnered? How many children do you want? By when do you want them? How will these goals fit in with and enhance your other goals and vice versa?

When it comes to the fourth Door of Success, *Enlightenment*, what are your goals? Do you have a spiritual path you are passionate about? Have you lapsed with regard to your path? Do you eschew organized religion in favor of personal spirituality? Are you opposed to religion and spirituality altogether, finding it hard to believe in the Divine, the Supernatural, or anything that hard science and evidence-based research cannot confirm? Wherever you are, the issue remains: what are your ultimate questions and answers about the meaning and purpose of life in general, and the meaning and purpose of your life in particular?

The best answers to these questions can be referred to as enlightenment. For some of us, this enlightenment means the ultimate reunion with our Divine Source; for others, it is the removal of all attack thoughts from the psyche; and for others still, it is ultimate peace, and so on.

Our purpose with this Door to Success is for us to have some explicitly stated goal about our connection to The Inner Genius and how we intend to continue to nurture this relationship for ever-greater and improving effectiveness, at a minimum, in living our lives.

Do you intend to visit some churches, mosques, or synagogues in the coming year? To read up on a spiritual classic? To go on a retreat? To work with a spiritual director? To embark on a new spiritual discipline of some kind? Write down your best answers to the "how much, by when, doing what" question for the Enlightenment Door to Success.

Recent Achievements

In the Recent Achievements box, you can fill in any recent achievements in the last six months. You can go further back if you'd like to a year or two or three for any recent achievements that will remind you that you're making progress. It does not matter how big or how small these achievements are. The main thing is that you note them down.

In my one-on-one executive coaching sessions, the first question I usually ask at the start of the session is, "What's better since we talked the last time?" The purpose of this question is to set the expectation for the coaching sessions that there is always some achievement between sessions worth celebrating.

In addition to setting up this expectation, the "What's better?" question is a form of mindtraining. As we ask and answer it over and again from coaching session to coaching session, our minds become increasingly able to see what is working in what we are doing. A client suggested I incorporate a section on The 1-Page Mind Trainer for celebrating achievements in the spirit of the "What's better?" question, and so this is how the Recent Achievements box came to be a part of The 1-Page Mind Trainer. This is a delightful aspect of developing a product for the marketplace, i.e., where the market tells you what features it would like to see in the product.

In the Recent Achievements box, list all your current achievements about the goals you've put in the Goals box, or any other problems you've been able to solve, or that you've made some inroads into.

The Parking Lot

Next is the Parking Lot box. Here, you want to enter in any goals you're interested in but are not ready to move on in the current quarter or even in the next several years.

For instance, you may have a goal to start a business, but see this as something you'll do 3-5 years from now. It is a good idea to have it in the Parking Lot box so you can keep it in view as you work to accomplish more immediate goals. Doing this can keep us from flitting about from thing to thing where one day we are all pumped up about an immediate goal, and then the next day we are shifting to some far-off goal. With this approach, we stay steadily focused on our immediate goals while also keeping in view goals that may be further off.

The Parking Lot box is another client-led addition to The 1-Page Mind Trainer. With earlier versions, I found clients stating, "Well, I'm currently in real estate, but I'm thinking of going to medical school and becoming a physician, so I've got some career transitions to make down the line, but I've got some real estate goals I'm working on right now—i.e., I want to put it in the Parking Lot that I'm on my way to becoming a physician." Such longer -term goals might be two or three years out in terms of when we're hoping to make the transition, so Parking Lot items are things that are on the horizon a little further out.

It's also a good idea to note goals down in terms of desired due dates that are as specific and concrete as possible. So, rather than say, "Two years from now, I'll achieve such and such....," say, "Okay, on January 1st, 20xx, I have achieved such and such ...." You want these goals to be measurable, you want them to be clear, and you want them to be ambitious.

Stress Box and Current Problems

In The Blueprint Key section of The 1-Page Mind Trainer, you have an area called the "Stress Box" and "Current Problems to Be Solved."

When we're considering The Blueprint Key to Miracle Success, you might recall that our foundational affirmation goes like this: *"I am aware of and undo my negative blueprints."* So first, you're going to list the different issues causing you stress in the current circumstances of your life then you're going to clean these out.

Continuing the example of switching from a real estate career to a medical career, an issue might be, "Well, it's a little late in the day to be thinking about doing this. I'm in my 30s, and I'm about to make this switch. It'll be another seven years of training, so I'll be in my late 30s when I finish my training and in my early 40s when I'm starting to build my practice, so the time factor is really stressing me out." Then there could be money concerns: "I've made a really nice living, and while I have some savings and investments, now I'm going to have to deplete most, if not all of that, taking out student loans, living the life of a student, being under this type of supervision, taking classes, tests, and all of that. Can I do it? Do I want to do it?" These are some of the stressors that could be affecting us as we consider pursuing such an important life's ambition.

We can also track the stressors that might concern us if we're a CEO, an executive, or an entrepreneur, for instance, in the quest to grow from a two-million-dollar a year business to a ten-million-dollar business or to create a billion-dollar fund with investment business.

In the Stress Box, one of our goals is to maintain an up-to-date and fresh inventory of the issues, concerns, challenges, and problems that weigh on us from day to day. The purpose this inventory is not to rehash or stay mired in the negatives but to turn them over to The Inner Genius for cleaning and deletion.

With the Stress Box, we are dealing with our negative blueprints, and more specifically, the best practices here are: a) to keep inventories of all the negatives we experience and b) to delete the negatives we experience, as well as the root causes of these negatives.

We've already talked about the highly effective cleaning or deletion method found in the ancient Hawaiian system known as Ho'oponopono. Just as a refresher, what you're doing when you look at your stressors and traumas here in the Stress box, is that you're repeating the 4 cleaning affirmations as incessantly as possible all day long. The 4 affirmations are *"I love you, I'm sorry, please forgive me, and thank you."* Or alternatively, these phrases can be rendered as *"I love you, I'm stuck, please delete my negative programming, and thank you."* I have found that, in working with my clients, the more traditional Ho'oponopono phrases are easier to understand in the slightly modified versions I've come up with. The goal here is not to replace the more traditional phrases with the ones I've come up with but rather to provide a quick way for us to remember what each phrase is achieving for us.

We say these affirmations to The Inner Genius, the Inner Buddha, the Inner Jesus, or the Holy Spirit in our higher mind, however you want to characterize this higher mind. We're not listing these stressors simply to list them. These are items to be cleaned on along with our cleaning on our goals as well. *"I love you, I'm sorry, please forgive me, and thank you,"* said over your stressors as well as your goals, will help to eliminate deeper blockages and the repeating patterns of self-sabotage that you're not really quite aware of, and this will help you move forward towards the success you seek and desire. This is all part of the miraculous breakthrough process.

As we repeat as incessantly as possible all day long the phrases *"I love you, I'm sorry, please forgive me, and thank you,"* here's a recap of what each phrase means and what each phrase is accomplishing for us.

I love you—we are saying this to The Inner Genius (or God, Higher Power, Jesus, Buddha, etc. within). It's like the phone call we make to computer tech support when we've tried everything and still can't get our computer working properly. Tech support does not normally call us; we have to initiate the call. Saying I love you to The Inner Genius is us initiating a call to Divine tech support to address all the glitches on our psychological hard drive that are causing our computer (our overall psyche) to malfunction and not achieve the goals we're aiming for.

I'm sorry (or I'm stuck)—this phrase, said to The Inner Genius, is an acknowledgment that we've got negative programming on our

psychological hard drive that is causing our psyche to glitch. Somewhat like in 12-step recovery programs, we're using this phrase to
acknowledge that we're powerless to fix the problems on our psychological hard drives and that we need the help of a Higher Power to
become free from our serious addiction to a malfunctioning psyche.
The use of this phrase is also like responding to tech support when
they ask, "Tell me more about the problem you're having with your
computer." We're explaining all the things that are not working well,
or that are going wrong, or that we're having difficulties and problems with.

Please forgive me (or Please delete my negative programming)—
this phrase gives the Higher Power within (i.e., The Inner Genius)
permission to undo the mindset issues causing our problems by
undoing the negative programming that is giving rise to the problem
in the first place. Using another metaphor here, it's like we have a
very nightmarish DVD stuck in our mental or psychological movie-
playing equipment. And, rather than holding on to this DVD and
keeping it stuck in place through our various psychological defenses,
we are asking tech support to help us eject this negative, destructive
DVD and replace it with an inspiring and empowering DVD, which
then positively transforms the movie of our lives. For reasons having
to do with the principles of free will, we can't have this negative
programming deleted from our hard drive (or this negative DVD
replaced with a positive DVD), unless we specifically ask for this to be
done for us by Higher Power, and also grant Higher Power the
permission to do this cleaning for us. This is a bit like when actual
computer tech support says to us, "Can I get on your computer
remotely and look around to see what to do to fix the problem?"

Thank you (or Thank you for getting me unstuck)—this phrase is
about us responding with gratitude and joy to there being such a
straightforward process by which Higher Power fixes the glitches we
are having and by which Higher Power does all the heavy lifting
involved if only we'll request the help. With computer tech support,
we are usually overjoyed and effusive in our expressions of gratitude
towards them when they solve a problem for us that just seemed

ridiculously impossible for us to solve. This expression of gratitude also reinforces in us a positive memory of the freedom our turning to Divine tech support has provided, which makes us more ready to turn quickly to Divine tech support again and again. In other words, Divine tech support does not really need our gratitude; our gratitude benefits us.

ACIM purports to be another process for cleaning our hard drives of accumulated toxicity, negativity, and glitches, and ultimately for undoing the malicious ego entirely. In my experience, and for those who are familiar with the New York City subway system, Ho'oponopono is akin to the express trains in New York City's subway system which skip stops and thereby help passengers cover large distances very fast, while ACIM is akin to the local trains, which stop at each station along the way and thereby provides a more detailed and thorough service. Or alternatively, Ho'oponopono is like a bachelor's degree, and ACIM is like a Ph.D. in cleaning up the negativity in our psyches. In other words, Ho'oponopono is a good introduction to cleaning, and ACIM is a much deeper education and training in the cleaning process for people who find themselves drawn to a more comprehensive and systematic method. In coaching sessions, especially early on with newer clients, it may not be possible, or even desirable, to attempt to unfold the intricate power and beauty of ACIM. At the same time, it is much easier to quickly introduce the four cleaning phrases of Ho'oponopono and see clients begin to benefit right away from using them.

Your Main Traumas

In the Main Traumas Box, our goal is to create an inventory of the scariest, most upsetting, and most difficult experiences we can remember. These can be about how we were parented—a place I like to start with clients when we are doing this part of the blueprint work. We can also be systematic about additional traumas by surfacing and recording any painful memories regarding health, wealth, love, and enlightenment.

When it comes to the Trauma Box, here's a quick rundown of some of my main ones to get you going with yours: my dad's alcohol and smoking; my parent's conflicts, being sent away to boarding school at ten years, and the bullying, squalor, and claustrophobia of that experience; my dad's political conflicts and various financial blows; some of my academic nightmares; finding my true stride and migrating from an undergrad in science, biology, and chemistry to, eventually, and with many steps in between, into a Ph.D. process focused on psychology and religion; having enormous difficulties with my German translation exam in the Ph.D. program but eventually breaking through on that miraculously; a whole bunch of stuff with nightmare relationships; and having a catastrophic diagnosis of congestive heart failure in 2014. Quite a collection of traumatic nightmares there.

The easiest way to start collecting your various traumas in a systematic and comprehensive manner is to think of three negative things about your father as a parent and three negative things about your mother as a parent that you experienced growing up as a child (or 3 negative things about anyone else who parented you). We are talking about your experiences of pain anywhere up until about ten years old.

Then if you want to go beyond the parental traumas, you can add on any other trauma: the first day at school, somebody bullying you, the first time you saw a dead body, your pet dying, a parent or another loved one dying, some crisis, catastrophe on the social scene, rumors of war, serial killers, mass shootings, or any of the things that we hear in the news that can be upsetting even to adults that you might have been picking up.

Again, our goal is not only to surface the painful material but to clean it from our psychological hard drive. Here is an illustration of how all the elements we have explored thus far come together to help us go from nightmares to miracles.

Your Genius Areas

In the Genius Areas Box, write down your areas of special talent and/or passion and what I refer to as your exponentials, which I'll be explaining more fully in a moment. In the Genius Areas box, one of our goals is to write down things that we are talented in, skilled in, or passionate about. These things often are what we consider to be our hobbies, and we consider them here in The 1-Page Mind Trainer with the added focus on them as objective measures or proxies of our progress in our growth and learning as leaders.

For me, a significant focus when it comes to what I write down in the Genius Areas Box is my study and teaching of *A Course in Miracles*. I find it the best teaching material on how to become a miracle worker and how to be miracle minded for oneself and the rest of the world, so I have ACIM written down in my Genius Areas Box.

I study ACIM day in and day out, all the time, thinking about it and internalizing its teachings. I feel connected to the voice that teaches within it, a voice that purports to be Jesus. I totally and fully believe and embrace that the voice teaching in ACIM is Jesus.

In a manner that is similar for you, I encourage you to write down what you are just as passionate and obsessed about in your own life —that represents your fascination with what you consider to be genius ability and special talent.

The other interest that I am passionate about that I have written down in the Genius Areas Box is my passion for guitar studies. I am not by any stretch a talented guitar player, but I do love studying the instrument. It keeps me honest with myself about whether I am applying my mindset teachings in my own personal life where I can measure my actual growth and progress regularly. With the guitar, either I'm improving as a guitarist, or I'm not.

For me, my main focus is on blues, jazz, and fusion guitar music. I have a list of songs in my current repertoire that I play every week. I focus on the chord progressions first, committing these to memory as quickly as possible. Then I play along with these songs often, using each time I go through the song as a type of mind-training to internalize the melody and the solo of the song more fully and organically in my psyche. Using various software programs, I can play with any accompaniment I choose. I can slow down fast solos and learn them note-by-note, practicing them at increasing speeds until I can play them back accurately. By using The 3 Keys Approach, I have begun to make breakthroughs in my playing that seemed impossible for me to achieve.

I supplement all the practicing with hypnosis programs and subliminal programs for learning to play the guitar, and I am amazed at my breakthroughs. Now, I'll readily admit that I am no Jimi Hendrix, George Benson, or Pat Metheny (yet, lol) but I do love this music very deeply. And, in a relatively brief period since applying The 3 Keys Program to my playing and studying, I have noticed exponential growth and improvement all-around in my musicianship. You could say that I have taken all I have learned trying to get through my German translation exam ordeal and applied the tools and techniques to other areas of my life that I've chosen to pursue and that I genuinely enjoy, but that I've been blocked in somehow. Other areas for me that I intend to include over time are ballroom dancing and yoga.

Now, as we gain confidence on an almost daily basis in developing our talents, skills, and passions for hobbies we've not been progressing very well in, we learn to transfer these skills to our leadership goals, our business goals, and our health, wealth, love, and enlightenment goals, desires, and challenges.

I recommend you have an area of special talent or passion that you hone and refine and use all of these tools and techniques to make improvements in.

For some people, it's golf; for others, it is chess, traveling around the world, gourmet cooking, or tennis. The main thing is to have your area, and then to dedicate to it or rededicate to it if you have lapsed, and then use all the miracle mindset teachings in this book to see how rapidly you can make improvements in your skill with your chosen interests.

Now back to the concept of exponentials, which I mentioned above. Exponentials refer to anything that gives us a huge return on investment, provides us with significant leverage, or helps us get amazing amounts of things done with minimal effort. One example that can stimulate us to think and behave exponentially is the way catalysts and enzymes work. Without them, chemical and biological reactions can take forever; with them, these same reactions can happen in nanoseconds. Or consider the world of astronomy and all the galaxies in the universe, and all the stars in those galaxies, and how vast this whole area is. For me, the whole study of billionaires is part of my fascination with exponentials.

How do some people (and here I am focused on people who are legal and ethical in what they do, as well as humane and philanthropic) figure out how to get to a billion dollars, ten billion dollars, or 50 billion dollars and beyond in personal wealth? How do they build multi-billion-dollar enterprises? I think these are all fascinating questions to consider in relation to the Genius Areas Box.

With regard to the Exponentials aspect of the Genius Areas box, our goal is to ruminate regularly on all forms of leverage that make sense to us. By this, I mean, we develop the habits of understanding, appreciating, using, and strengthening our skills in using tools and techniques in life that provide us with enormous leverage.

Another example I use a lot with my clients is that of having a car jack in your car for when you have a flat tire. With the car jack, you can lift the car off the ground and replace the flat tire in about 30 minutes or less. Without the jack, you cannot perform this task. The jack is the key to the "miracle" of being able to lift the car off the ground and replace the tire – I call this type of power *exponential power*.

For another example of exponential power, let's consider various digital technologies, such as our computers, our tablets, our smartphones, and our apps. We get how the digital revolution, for the most part, enables us to be vastly more productive and efficient in most of the things we do these days. That is one way of thinking of things exponentially and bringing that kind of thinking into your 1-Page

Mind Trainer on a daily basis. As an example of digital tech exponentials in action, let's consider the use of email. If I have an email list of, say, 1 million people all over the world, I can easily compose a message and send it to all of them, and I can do this quickly on a regular basis every time I want to communicate with my community. These recurring tasks related to messaging my million-person community would be almost impossible to achieve if I was using snail mail.

The digital revolution has brought such leveraged or exponential ability into almost every area of our work and personal lives: booking airline tickets, hotels, rental cars, and entertainment, and trends in such exponential directions are only going to increase and explore even more. Almost all of us are aware of this superfast and evolving process. What we seem to be less aware of is the internal aspects of what is reflected externally in all these converging and overlapping exponentials: namely, all the superpowers we possess internally, in our psyches, through The Inner Genius, and which we can unleash and harness for miracle results in health, wealth, love, and enlightenment.

Your Miracle Resume

Here you're going to list all the miraculous things that have happened in your life. It's best to do this miracle inventory in decades, so from your first ten years, then from ten to 20, then from 20 to 30, then from 30 to 40 and so on.

In the Miracle Resume box, we are listing the most amazing, fortuitous, synchronistic, and/or miraculous experiences we have had since early childhood. While we may have many such stories, our goal here is to have 1 or 2 solid ones for each decade of our lives. All the other stories are valuable and, as with the information we have been capturing for each of the other boxes, can be documented in full elsewhere.

Remember, because we are compressing all these boxes onto our universal 1-Page Mind Trainer and then using this 1-Page Mind

Trainer as a crucial part of our daily regimen, we will be seeing our miracle resume and the miracle story headlines in it on a regular basis. This will instill in us a deep inner knowing that because we have experienced such amazing opportunities, breakthroughs, healing, rescue, salvation, or epiphanies and realizations before in our lives, even before we really might have known anything about the miraculous explicitly, we are in in a much better position to experience even more miracles on a daily basis, whether it's with our goals and achievements, or with our problems, our stressors, and our traumas.

Here is the list of my top miracles since childhood, some of which I have already discussed:

- Practical: My attending Yale
- Blueprint: Me Passing German + Completing My Ph.D.
- Inner Genius: My Wisdom Figure Dream
- Health: My Healed Heart Miracle (Life from Death) + Eliminating Smoking and Drinking
- Wealth: My Billionaire Life Miracles & Results
- Love: My Escape from Nightmare Relationships
- Enlightenment: My Spiritual Awakening

In The Practical Area, one of my earliest miracles was coming to Yale from Ghana. I started planning that process when I was 16, and a year later, despite many obstacles and a couple of discouraging voices, I made it. In The Blueprint Area, one of my most significant miracles was passing my German scholarly translation exam, which was a bear of a thing to get through.

Then along the way in terms of The Inner Genius part of my miracle resume, I had an amazing dream about a wisdom figure, like an angel, like an Einstein (who promised to teach me everything about quantum physics). This figure appeared to me like a Jesus figure who promised to show me and teach me about the miraculous and was really quite a powerful miracle worker. That dream still keeps me connected to angelic figures in literature and in various films to this day. Also, as a result of that dream, I see various super-hero figures in cartoons, TV, and film as contemporary versions of what people used to rely on (and still do) regarding angels with their various superpowers.

The Health area of my miracle resume has to do primarily with the miracle I experienced regarding the healing of my heart, as well as my being able to quit drinking and smoking several years before my heart episode.

The Wealth part of my miracle resume has to do with getting my own life into a state of financial flow and security. It also has to do with several key breakthroughs in supporting my aspiring billionaire clients with their billionaire goals, for example.

The Love part of my miracle resume is primarily about my escape from nightmare relationships that were bound to be the death of me had I not gotten out of them.

The Enlightenment part of my miracle resume has to do with my spiritual awakening when I was 20 years old as an undergrad in college.

Other Affirmations

In addition the various boxes we have looked at above, and how to go about filling these boxes in, there are several affirmations on the 1-Page Mind Trainer.

There are affirmations for each of The 3 Keys:

- For The Practical Key: *"I set and achieve clear, ambitious and measurable goals."*
- For The Blueprint Key: *"I am aware of and undo my negative blueprints."*
- For The Inner Genius Key: *"I am aware of and use the guidance, strength, and plan of The Inner Genius in what I think, say, and do."*

There are affirmations for each of the 4 Doors:

- For The Health Door: *"I now manifest and enjoy optimal health in all areas of my life."*
- For The Wealth Door: *"I am now a miracle-minded enterprise leader"* (or executive, entrepreneur, millionaire, billionaire, head of state/politician or somebody who works closely with them, CEO, celebrity, mover and shaker, etc.)
- For The Love Door: *"I now manifest and enjoy my optimal holy relationship with_____ ."* You can include here people you are in a romantic relationship with, friends, family, even your enemies.
- For The Enlightenment Door: *"I am enlightened, and I now manifest and enjoy optimal peace."*

I review these affirmations at the start of my day as part of my daily mind training regimen.

Also, you will find in this box my favorite definition of miracles, which is as follows: *"Miracles are solutions to problems that seem impossible to solve"* (adapted from Lesson 50 in ACIM). I use this affirmation at the very beginning of my daily 30-minute exercise routine to remind myself that my principal core value is organized around the word "miracle." Doing this reminds me that what I'm seeking for myself are miracles in my Health (my heart, toes, teeth, for example), Wealth (my SynchroMind and Billionaire Life coaching businesses), Love (love towards, and peace with, all people), and Enlightenment (seeing the Divine light in myself and in all others, and eliminating all the attack and separation thoughts in my mind, and supporting the rest of the world to do the same).

During the practice periods at the beginning of the day when I am reviewing and meditating on my 1-Page Mind Trainer before my day really gets going, I am orienting myself towards a super-strong connection with The Inner Genius, and thus seeking the "fastest, easiest, and smartest ways" to achieve my goals, through the Divine Higher Power we all have within us. I'm not aiming for these results through my ego, which will only hurt me and causes me to struggle and suffer needlessly. The sentence completion exercise I've put on the 1-Page Minder trainer reads as follows: **"For Miracles, Ask the Inner Genius: 'What's the fastest, easiest, and smartest way for me to _____?'"** Then plug into the end of the sentence whatever it is you are seeking guidance and strength from The Inner Genius to accomplish in a miracle-minded way. Here are some examples of the completed sentence with our question for The Inner Genius:

"What's the fastest, easiest, and smartest way for me to heal from this cancer?"

"What's the fastest, easiest, and smartest way for me to grow my business to $50 million a year?"

"What's the fastest, easiest, and smartest way for me to find and partner with my soul mate?"

"What's the fastest, easiest, and smartest way for me to become enlightened?"

Doing these types of sentence completions reminds me of the source of the miraculous results I'm aiming for every time I look at the 1-Page Mind Trainer.

Then there is the affirmation from ACIM Lesson 77, "I am entitled to miracles," which reinforces the focus on miracles, and then finally, there is the reminder from Lesson 97 to practice tapping into Divine Miracle Power at least five5 minutes of every hour throughout the day beyond the initial preparation for the day.

Taken all together, I liken all these aspects of The 1-Page Mind Trainer to the aspects of a pilot's pre-flight check plan. It is a good idea to go through everything before pushing back from the airport terminal and moving towards the runway for final takeoff. And then, once in flight, to keep monitoring and tweaking everything consistently throughout the rest of the flight to ensure that the plane remains on the desired course. This is a metaphor for how we can approach our journey through each day: with clear intention, preparation, and practice to make each day a day of miracles in our personal and business lives.

CHAPTER 8

DAILY MIND-TRAINING

T-12.II.4.Remember what was said about the frightening perceptions of little children, which terrify them because they do not understand them. p218 2 If they ask for enlightenment and accept it, their fears vanish. 3 But if they hide their nightmares, they will keep them. 4 It is easy to help an uncertain child, for he recognizes that he does not understand what his perceptions mean. 5 Yet you believe that you do understand yours. 6 Little child, you are hiding your head under the cover of the heavy blankets you have laid upon yourself. 7 You are hiding your nightmares in the darkness of your own false certainty and refusing to open your eyes and look at them.
—**A Course in Miracles, T-12.II.4**

Now that you have compiled your 1-Page Daily Mind Trainer, your goal is to get in the habit of using it daily as part of your Daily Mind Training Regime.

21-Day Miracle Campaign

Develop a daily regimen to use at the start of your day in which you engage in 21 straight days of mental rehearsal using guided meditation, visualization, and/or self-hypnosis audio programs.

Use a calendar on the wall, and put a tick, cross, or other symbol on it each day that you complete your Morning Miracle Rehearsal.

Your goal is to create an unbroken 21-day campaign. If you miss a day, you just restart from Day 1.

Once you have completed the 21-Day campaign, chances are you will not want to lose your winning focus, and you will be more motivated than ever to incorporate the Morning Miracle Rehearsal regimen into your routine in an ongoing way.

I Am Entitled to Miracles

Begin your Morning Miracle Rehearsal with the affirmation, *"I am entitled to miracles."*

This is the underlying approach to my waking up from my traumatic nightmare with congestive heart failure. This method can apply to any other nightmare, trauma, disaster, challenge, problem, or goal in our lives.

Be aware, though, that this is not the kind of entitlement that expects results without practice. You are entitled to miracles, but they are not going to happen automatically without your inviting them, preparing for them, welcoming them, and celebrating them when they manifest for you.

Make the Mind Trainer Yours

Don't be afraid to tweak The 1-Page Mind Trainer to reflect your own beliefs and personality. You can make The 1-Page Mind Trainer yours simply by adding your goals, achievements, stresses and traumas, genius, talents, and miracles.

Or, if you're creatively minded, you might want to turn your 1-Page Mind Trainer into a full-fledged vision board; or make it into a more elaborate digital version that you update regularly, that includes a meditation track or other mind training tools. Also if you do all this digitally in PowerPoint or some other program you prefer, it will make updating your 1-Page Mind Trainer regularly very simple. It also makes it a lot easier to design many different 1-Pagers quickly for different areas of your life, as well as to update them frequently so that they stay fresh and relevant.

If the affirmations on The 1-Page Mind Trainer do not resonate with you, you might want to replace them with altered versions, remembering to keep them in the present tense and frame them in a positive way.

Again, these are just suggestions. Nothing here is written in stone. You can modify the various categories, tweaking them, adding things, adding your own pictures, little clues here and there, triggers that will remind you of other powerful truths and principles to keep you focused, inspired, and motivated about executing on your 1-Page Mind Trainer.

Incorporate affirmations for your optimal health, successful work and financial prosperity, loving relationships, and spiritual enlightenment onto your 1-Page Mind Trainer, and as you proceed with your 21-Day Campaign, continue tweaking and refining everything on the 1-Page Mind Trainer. Doing this type of tweaking and continuous improvement makes the whole process more and more powerful and effective; it all becomes a virtuous circle.

Also, feel free to extend your 21-Day Miracle Campaign to 60 days or even 90 days, and capture your evolving insights onto your 1-Page Mind Trainer and in your journal as you go along.

Home In on Your Goals

You may have an extensive goals list in each of the Health, Wealth, Love, and Enlightenment areas. The goals you initially chose for your Goals Grid and 1-Page Mind Trainer might not be the goals you want or need to work on as you proceed and grow more involved with developing your miracle mindset .

Often when we first start doing intensive psychological and spiritual work, all manner of blocks come to the surface, and the things we thought were our biggest priorities turn out to be distractions thrown in our way by the malicious ego.

Do not be afraid to change your goals or to refine them as your understanding grows.

When it comes to your goals, mostly remember the affirmation, "I set and achieve clear, ambitious, and measurable goals."

Work on Your Blueprints

When it comes to doing your blueprint work, you can always remind yourself what the essence of this aspect of developing a miracle mindset is by repeating this foundational affirmation frequently: "I am aware of and undo my negative blueprints."

Read through your blueprints, and clean on them using the Ho'oponopono mantras.

"I love you, I am stuck, please delete my negative programming, and thank you for getting me unstuck."

Or if you prefer them, here are the original versions of the cleaning affirmations:

"I love you, I am sorry, please forgive me, and thank you."

Commit to Partnering with The Inner Genius

As part of your 21-Day Miracle Campaign, commit to having complete reliance on the guidance, strength, and plan of The Inner Genius in everything you think, say, and do, and capture this commitment on your vision board.

As part of your Morning Miracle Rehearsal, after you have cleaned on your blueprints, say the affirmation, *"I am aware of and use the guidance, strength, and plan of The Inner Genius of what I think, say, and do."*

When you have finished chanting the Ho'oponopono mantras on your blueprints, ask your Inner Genius, "What are the fastest, easiest, and smartest ways to overcome my negative programs and reach my goals today?"

One of the more powerful approaches to embrace about miracles and developing and having a miracle mindset is to ask The Inner Genius for clarity about what you are aiming for. Here are some examples that you can easily modify to suit you and your goals:

What is the fastest, easiest, and smartest way for me to achieve optimal health in all areas of my life?

What is the fastest, easiest, and smartest way for me to become a successful, miracle minded enterprise leader?

What is the fastest, easiest, and smartest way for me to get to my first ten million in business (or my first million dollars, or my first billion dollars)?

What is the fastest, easiest, and smartest way for me to achieve peaceful loving relationships with all people?

What is the fastest, easiest, and smartest way for me to achieve spiritual maturity?

Stay Connected

Look at and meditate on your 1-Page Mind Trainer every day as part of your daily regimen to prepare for the day. Stay connected to it throughout the day and reflect on it before sleep at the end of the day.

Remember to incorporate these best practices into your Morning Miracle Rehearsal:

1. Regulated breathing
2. Progressive relaxation
3. Guided imagery
4. Positive self-talk

Hypnosis programs and guided imagery programs help with this rehearsal tremendously.

Keep developing ways of stacking the various tools, techniques, and concepts presented here through a meditation practice of five minutes every hour. In other words, train yourself to rehearse and practice incessantly for miracles in every area of your life at the beginning of the day, throughout the day, and at the end of the day.

Just as a reminder, the reason we focus on miracles in all of this is that miracles are solutions to problems that seem impossible to solve. Unfortunately, the alternative (i.e., not rehearsing for miracles incessantly) leads to nightmares.

Conclusion

You now have a program designed to enable you to manifest miracles in your life on a daily basis.

The 3 Keys to Miracle Success reflect for The **Practical, Blueprint**, and **Inner Genius** areas of the psyche and empower you to open The 4 Doors to Miracle Success in **Health, Wealth, Love, and Enlightenment.**

Whether you approach the miraculous through a scientific, psychological, or religious lens and belief system or some combination of these, you have The Integrated Model of the Psyche that allows you to plug in your existing beliefs and frameworks.

You also know what mind training is, and you have a range of mind training tools you can practice with; and you can also continue to explore mind training in new ways in order to add to your mind training toolkit.

The Goals Grid is a place to list all your goals, negative programs, and insights in each of The 4 Doors so that you can:

1. Set your goals.
2. Undo your negative blueprints through cleaning.
3. Leverage The Inner Genius to astronomically enhance your goal-setting-achieving and the cleaning.

The 1-Page Mind Trainer is your pre-flight check, GPS, work-bench, and dojo, if you like. It is where you show up every morning for your Morning Miracle Rehearsal, clock in, do the work, and check your progress. It is where you face your nightmares, clean and heal your wounds, and incubate and document miracles.

Using a 21-Day Miracle Campaign will help you more fully to install your new miracle mindset which will help you turn your Nightmares into Miracles.

REFERENCES

Books

- Allen, Judy Edwards. (1992). *The Five Stages of Getting Well.* Portland: LifeTime Publishing.
- Asomaning, David C. (2018). *Signs and Wonders: The Relationship Between Synchronicity and the Miraculous in Depth Psychology and Religion.* SynchroMind.
- Bennington, Emily and Marianne Williamson. (2017). *Miracles at Work: Turning Inner Guidance into Outer Influence.* Sounds True.
- Bolles, Richard N. and Katherine Brooks. (2021). *What Color Is Your Parachute? 2021: Your Guide to a Lifetime of Meaningful Work and Career Success.* Ten Speed Press.
- Chernow, Ron. (2011). *Washington: A Life.* Penguin Books.
- Collins, Jim. (2011). *Good to Great: Why Some Companies Make the Leap...And Others Don't.* Harper Business.
- Collins, Jim and Jerry I. Porras. (2011). *Built to Last: Successful Habits of Visionary Companies.* Harper Business.

- Covey, Stephen. (2013). *The 7 Habits of Highly Effective People: Powerful Lessons in Personal Change.* Simon & Schuster.
- Diamandis, Peter H. and Stephen Kotler. (2012). *Abundance: The Future Is Better Than You Think.* Free Press.
- Dispenza, Joe. (2017). *Becoming Supernatural: How Common People Are Doing the Uncommon.* Hay House Inc.
- Dweck, Carol S. *(2006). Mindset: The New Psychology of Success.* Random House.
- Foundation for Inner Peace. (1992). *A Course in Miracles*: Combined Volume. Foundation for Inner Peace.
- Freud, Sigmund. (2019). *The Ego and the Id.* Clydesdale.
- Goldsmith, Marshall, Laurence S. Lyons and Sarah McArthur. (2012). *Coaching for Leadership: Writings on Leadership from the World's Greatest Coaches.* Pfeiffer.
- Hall, Stacy and Jan Brogniez. (2001). *Attracting Perfect Customers: The Power of Strategic Synchronicity.* Berrett-Koehler Publishers.
- Harnish, Verne. (2014). *Scaling Up: How a Few Companies Make It...and Why the Rest Don't (Rockefeller Habits 2.0).* Gazelles, Inc.
- Hendrix, Harville and Helen LaKelly Hunt. (2019). *Getting the Love You Want: A Guide for Couples.* St. Martin's Griffin.
- Hill, Napoleon and Arthur Pell. (2005). *Think and Grow Rich: The Landmark Bestseller—Now Revised and Updated for the 21st Century.* Tarcher.
- Isaacson, Walter. (2014). *The Innovators: How a Group of Inventors, Hackers, Geniuses, and Geeks Created the Digital Revolution.* Thorndike Press.
- Ismail, Salim, Michael S. Malone, Yuri van Geest, and Peter H. Diamandis. (2014). *Exponential Organizations: Why New Organizations Are Ten Times Better, Faster, and Cheaper Than Yours (and What To Do About It).* Diversion Books.
- Jaworski, Joseph. (2011). *Synchronicity: The Inner Path of Leadership.* Berrett-Koehler Publishers.

- Jung, Carl G, Sonu Shamdasani and R.F.C. Hull. (2012). *Synchronicity: An Acausal Connecting Principle.* Princeton University Press.
- Odell, Catherine M. (2017). *Father Solanus Casey, Revised and Updated.* Our Sunday Visitor, Inc.
- Peale, D. N. V. (1990). *The Power of Positive Thinking.* Cedar Books.
- Renard, Gary. (2004).*The Disappearance of the Universe: Straight Talk about Illusions, Past Lives, Religion, Sex, Politics, and the Miracles of Forgiveness.* Hay House.
- Roman, Sanaya and Duane Packer. (1988). *Creating Money: Keys to Abundance.* HJ Kramer.
- Sviokla, John and Mitch Cohen. (2014). *The Self-made Billionaire Effect: How Extreme Producers Create Massive Value.* Portfolio.
- Tinkham, Pamela, Linda Mortenson, and Nadja Fidelia. (2017). *Healing Trauma from the Inside Out: Practices from the East and West.* Pamela Tinkham, LLC.
- Turner, Kelly A. (2014). *Radical Remission: Surviving Cancer Against All Odds.* HarperCollins.
- Ulanov, Ann. (2019). *The Psychoid, Soul and Psyche: Piercing Space-Time Barriers.* Daimon.
- Vitale, Joe and Ihaleakala Hew Len. (2009). *Zero Limits: The Secret Hawaiian System for Wealth, Health, Peace, and More.* Wiley.
- Wimbush, Vincent. Ed. (2001). *African Americans and the Bible: Sacred Texts and Social Structures.* Continuum.

Movies

- *It's a Wonderful Life*
- *Limitless*
- *Miracles from Heaven*
- *The Bishop's Wife*

- *The Preachers Wife*

TV Shows

- *Highway to Heaven*
- *Touched By an Angel*

APPENDIX

Affirmations
- https://www.louisehay.com/affirmations/

Guided Imagery
- https://www.healthjourneys.com/

Visualization
- https://www.makeavisionboard.com/what-is-a-vision-board/
- https://www.mindmovies.com/
- https://www.mindmovies.com/products/matrix_info.php
- https://www.subliminalvisionboards.com/

Meditation
- https://www.headspace.com/
- https://www.calm.com/

Subliminals and Triliminals
- https://youtu.be/MdV2XWc75Uk
- https://subliminal360.com/

Hypnosis
- https://www.hypnosisdownloads.com

Mindfulness
- https://www.mindful.org

ACIM
- http://acim.org/

Ho'oponopono
- https://www.hooponoponocertification.com/
- https://apple.co/3wt5Yo8

Brain Entrainment
- https://www.spiritualtechnologies.io/
- http://www.iawaketechnologies.com/
- https://www.centerpointe.com/
- http://finderscourse.com/

VR
- https://guidedmeditationvr.com/

Nootropics
- https://onlinelibrary.wiley.com/doi/abs/10.1002/ddr.430020505)
- https://observer.com/2021/01/best-nootropics/

ABOUT THE AUTHOR

Dave Asomaning is the founder of SynchroMind, a leadership development company dedicated to helping businesses, teams, and individuals transform adversity into opportunity through miracle-minded executive coaching, consulting, mastermind seminar programs, online courses, and private groups.

SynchroMind works with a diverse set of clients in business, education, government, healthcare, religion and spirituality, the media, and sports and entertainment, and with individuals and teams ranging from aspiring leaders to those who are highly experienced, have high net worth, and also have significant influence.

At the core of SynchroMind is Dave's "3 Keys to Miracle Success" operating system, a method that has helped transform hundreds of lives over the last 25 years. With his book *Nightmares to Miracles*, Dave shares this system with a simple, easy-to-follow approach designed to help everyone who desires to upgrade their lives.

Dave Asomaning is a graduate of Yale University, where he majored in biology. He went on to earn an M.A. from Hartford Seminary and an M.Div. from the Yale Divinity School, together with a diploma in Anglican Studies from Berkeley Divinity School at Yale, and a teaching certificate from Southern Connecticut State University. He also received clinical training in individual, family, and group psychotherapy and spirituality at The Blanton-Peale Graduate Institute, where his clinical work focused on synchronicity and the miraculous. He completed an M.Phil. and a Ph.D. in depth psychology (psychoanalysis) and religion, with a dissertation entitled, *Signs and Wonders: The Relationship Between Synchronicity and the Miraculous in*

Depth Psychology and Religion at Union Theological Seminary in New York City. This dissertation is the basis of Dave's first book, published in 2018.

Passionate about community and helping others, he has served in the Episcopal Church, as well as at Riverside Church in New York City. His hobbies include studying all kinds of guitar music (especially blues, jazz, and fusion), reading, watching movies, and traveling.

To learn more about Dave and his approach and experience, visit SynchroMind.com. You can also find him on most social media platforms.

ALSO BY THE AUTHOR

Inquire about any of the following offerings by emailing me here:

dasomaning@synchromind.com

Here's the link you can use to sign up for my monthly newsletter. In return, you will receive my FREE 9-page guide to The 3 Keys to Miracle Success which are a significant foundation for this book:

https://bit.ly/340yklV

Here's the link to the worksheets and graphics for this book:

https://bit.ly/3tmMMjx

(password: n2m)

Here's the website for my Nightmares to Miracles executive coaching, online course, and book:

https://nightmarestomiracles.com/

You are welcome to join the FREE Facebook Group for my Nightmares to Miracles book, online course, and coaching:

https://www.facebook.com/groups/nightmarestomiraclescoaching

Here's the link to my podcast:

https://www.synchromind.com/podcast

Here's the link to my first book, *Signs and Wonders*:

https://nightmarestomiracles.com/signs-and-wonders-book (please leave me a review on Amazon if you can—thank you!)

Printed in Poland
by Amazon Fulfillment
Poland Sp. z o.o., Wrocław